The Art of Choosing

The **Art** *of* **Choosing**

Carlos G. Valles, S.J.

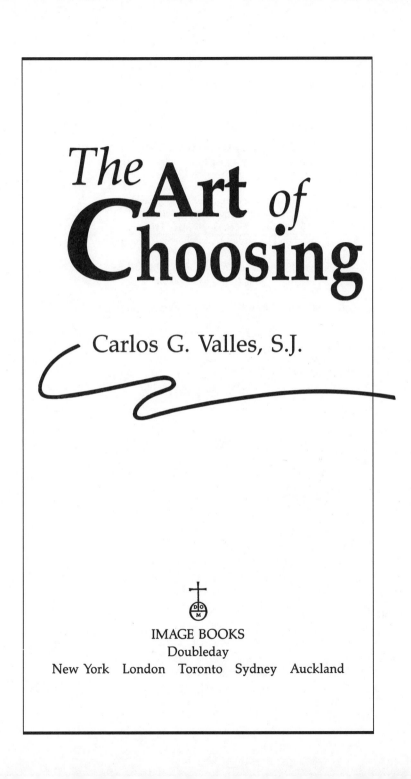

IMAGE BOOKS
Doubleday
New York London Toronto Sydney Auckland

AN IMAGE BOOK

Published by Doubleday, a division of
Bantam Doubleday Dell Publishing Group, Inc.
666 Fifth Avenue, New York, New York 10103

IMAGE, DOUBLEDAY, and the portrayal of
a cross intersecting a circle
are trademarks of Doubleday, a division of
Bantam Doubleday Dell Publishing Group, Inc.

Originally published in India by X. Diaz del Rio, S.J.,
Gujarat Sahitya Prakash.

This edition published by special arrangement with the author.

IMPRIMI POTEST: A. Sankoorikal, S.J.
Prov. of Gujarat
Jan. 28, 1986

IMPRIMATUR: + C. Gomes, S.J.
Bishop of Ahmedabad
Jan. 30, 1986

LIBRARY OF CONGRESS CATALOGING-IN-PUBLICATION DATA

Valesa, Father, 1925–
    The art of choosing / Carlos G. Valles.— 1st Image Books ed.
    p. cm.
    1. Decision-making (Ethics) I. Title.
BJ1419.V35 1989
241—dc19   89-1072
                                                        CIP

Book design by Patrice Fodero

September 1989
First Image Books Edition
DH

Contents

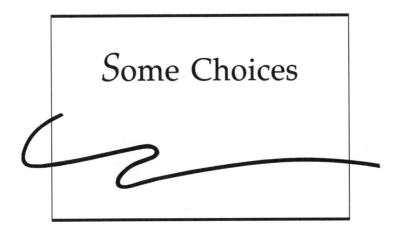

Some Choices

When I told a friend I was writing a book on how to make choices, he cut me short and said categorically, "That's very simple: First listen very carefully to what all others have to say about it. And then go and do what you damn well want."

I told him that the idea, almost the very expression, though in a different idiom, sounded familiar. It didn't take me long to locate the quotation. "Examine everything, and then hold on to what is best." That was Paul to his Thessalonians (1 Thess. 5:19). Valid precedent.

That idea sums up the whole book. Only that it takes some time—and often a lot of courage and wisdom and freedom—to come to know what one really wants, what is actually best for me and for all in the multiple choices of daily life, what is the will of God for me in practice today. So the book is there after all.

I heard that Pandit Nehru, when dealing as Prime Minister of India with Church representatives to learn their needs and their stand in controverted matters, said once with insight and respect: "One thing about these Christians. They know what they want." Beautiful definition from the beloved Pandit: A Christian is a man who knows what he wants. The gift of the Spirit.

To choose is to live, and as I understand and refine my ways of choosing and deciding and making up my mind, I understand better and refine more effectively my own life. This applies to the private life of the individual as well as to the common life of the group. The art of discerning is the art of living, and the practice of discernment with tact and sensitivity is the best way to revitalize a group and each one of its members. If an apostolic group wants to live and act as a group, it has to make an effort to learn how to think, plan, and decide things in common. This is not an easy task, but it definitely will prove most rewarding, as it can give a new unity, a common purpose, and a shared action to the group; and that is the best renewal a group can ever experience. The thought that this book might help in this task has given me joy while writing it.

Carlos G. Valles, S.J.
St. Xavier's College,
Ahmedabad, 380 009
India

The Need to Know

I've taken quite a few days to make up my mind about the subject of this book. I was almost getting nervous about it. I had several books in mind, some even boldly announced on the flap of previous publications of mine as being "In Preparation" (pure publicity stunt, as nothing is prepared); and others taking shape unbidden in the recesses of my mind as events took place and ideas occurred. I had finished my previous book, had taken a break to recover from the ordeal, and knew I had to come back to the old desk sooner or later for a new brainchild. And as I write only one book at a time, I had to fix clearly and definitely what this one would be. I cannot start writing unless I know what I'm writing about. I reviewed the list of possible topics, and on a first instinctive choice narrowed it down to two. But these two were neck and neck. I couldn't, for the life of me, choose one or the other. And the choice was important. I knew full well that if I made the wrong choice, started on it, and later inevitably realized I'd taken the wrong road, I would be helplessly stuck; that I would lose all inspiration and capacity to write, and would at the same time be stubbornly reluctant to leave the book once begun, knowing that if I interrupted it I would never finish it. I have had such experiences before. The right choice would lead me to two good books; the wrong one would ruin both. I knew it and I didn't want to make a mistake. I delayed the decision.

Suddenly one day I woke up in the morning with an idea so clear and evident and containing the obviously right solution that I smiled to myself. The topic of one of the books (this one) was to be how to make decisions. And that was exactly what I was doing in full earnestness and consciousness and pain and risk. I was in the process of making a decision—that is, I was already heart and soul in the midst of my book, in its subject, in its problem; I was living with full intensity the situation on which I wanted to shed light in this book. I had only to begin writing. I did. And as I began, I experienced that inner joy and spiritual contentment that are the heavenly confirmation of a right choice. I wrote on.

Choices are what make a man. They shape his personality, define his character, and make up his life. I am what my choices are, and so I want to know what they are, how I make them, how far my choices are my choices and not mere mimicry or weak subservience. The human act. The personal commitment. The free election. Never am I more I than when I stand serene, survey the field, weigh my choices, set my face in one direction and advance with firm step and joyful heart. To know what I want and to do it is the essence of life.

For a religious person the quest of the right choice takes on a new and much deeper dimension as the quest of God's will for him or for her. Once I have faith in God, I want to know that what I do is what he wants me to do. Jesus' ultimate satisfaction was "I do always what pleases him (the Father)"; and that is, in due proportion and humble imitation, the endeavor, the hope, the prize of every enlightened believer. To do his will for me.

The Need to Know

To do his will for me, I have to know what that will is. I know his commandments and his injunctions, I've listened to his prophets and his priests (and even to his canonists and moralists), I know what he expects of me in my moral life, and only my passions and attachments prevent me at times from doing what I know he wants me to do. But apart from morality or immorality, apart from right or wrong, apart from heaven or hell, I have a thousand daily choices, and sometimes big decisions in life, in which both options are legal and moral and valid—and yet I have to choose one and leave the other. Which? Which is more pleasing to God? Which does he really want? Which is his will for me?

Religious-minded people have used what means they knew, in the context and the culture in which they lived, to ascertain somehow the divine pleasure, the will of God, the shape of the future to guide their choices and direct their lives. Even divination of the future, in all its clumsy and sophisticated ways, is only an attempt to know what is going to happen, what God is going to do with the world and with me in it; and to adapt in consequence my doings to the course of events. This is for some, indeed for many, fate, karma, blind predestination of rigid events that leave hardly any room for personal freedom and spontaneous choices. There is a popular belief in India that the graph-like seams between the bones of the skull are the hieroglyphic writings that contain in cipher the whole history of the skull's owner from birth to death. Nobody, of course, has the key to the code, and in any case the writings appear only safely well after the person's death and in the privacy of the tomb— such is the typical and purposely muddled way of all prophetic divination and fortune-telling. The lines on the palm of the hand are more easily available for observation and, as such, have prompted a generous literature and provided almost a way of life to itinerant gypsies and professional palmists in all ages and in all latitudes. The lifeline in my

3

right hand says that I'm going to live ninety-two years, suffer a health breakdown at seventy-nine, and achieve the peak of my existence at seventy-four—that is, according to a friend of mine who practices palmistry and volunteered to read my hand free of charge. According to another, however, who again and again scrutinized my hand with a puzzled look, I should have been dead long ago. The funny thing is that in spite of such obvious conflict, and of my rationalistic approach and my total skepticism in the matter of palmistry, astrology, futurology, and black magic, I've somehow come to take for granted that I'm going to live ninety-two years as though that were an article of faith, a private revelation fixed and unchangeable. Maybe that is only a projection of my desire to live long, and maybe it is an irrational offshoot of the hidden tendency each person has to believe in the occult. I have pious religious friends who unfailingly read their horoscope—and often those of others!—every week. It provides a lot of fun—and a sidelight on the working of their minds.

When I visited the Holy Land years ago, I made it a point to go to Endor. I guess it is not a favorite spot with pilgrims, but I remembered the uncanny incident that took place there. King Saul had banished all witches from the land, as required by the law of the Lord; but he found himself in dire straits, about to lose his kingdom and his life, and with no prophet to consult, as Samuel was dead and the like of him had not arisen after him. So he went at night in disguise to the witch who had remained in hiding at Endor, and said to her: "Tell me my fortunes by consulting the dead, and call up the man I name to you." She hesitated, remonstrated, feared, recognized the king and reminded him of his ban on witches; finally she yielded and the ghost of Samuel appeared wrapped in a cloak. "Why have you disturbed me and brought me up? Why do you inquire from me now that the Lord has turned from you and become your adversary? The Lord will let your people Israel fall into the hands of the

Philistines, and tomorrow you and your sons will be with me." The next day Saul and his three sons lay dead on Mount Gilboa, "and the Philistines sent messengers through the length and breadth of their land to take the good news to idols and people alike" Endor had marked an important point in Saul's life, and I visited it. I saw no ghost.

The ephod, urim, and thummim formed part of the vestments of Aaron and of the liturgy of the Temple, and were regularly used, we don't exactly know how, to "consult the Lord," to find his will and pierce the veil of the future. "The Philistines were fighting against Keilah and plundering the threshing-floors; and when David heard this, he consulted the Lord and asked whether he should go and attack the Philistines. The Lord answered, 'Go, attack them, and relieve Keilah.' But David's men said to him, 'As we are now, we have enough to fear from Judah. How much worse if we challenge the Philistine forces at Keilah!' David consulted the Lord once again and the Lord answered him, 'Go to Keilah; I will give the Philistines into your hands.' So David and his men went to Keilah and fought the Philistines; they carried off their cattle, inflicted a heavy defeat on them and relieved the inhabitants. Abiathar son of Ahimelech made good his escape and joined David at Keilah, bringing the ephod with him. Saul was told that David had entered Keilah, and he said, 'God has put him into my hands; for he has walked into a trap by entering a walled town with gates and bars.' He called out the levy to march on Keilah and besiege David and his men. When David learned that Saul planned his undoing, he told Abiathar the priest to bring the ephod, and then he prayed. 'O Lord God of Israel, I thy servant have heard news that Saul intends to come to Keilah and destroy the city because of me. Will the citizens of Keilah surrender me to him? Will Saul come as I have heard? O Lord God of Israel, I pray thee, tell thy servant.' The Lord answered, 'He will come.' Then David asked, 'Will the citizens of Keilah surrender me and my men to Saul?,' and the Lord answered, 'They will.' Then David left Keilah at once with his men, who numbered about six hundred, and moved about from place to place. When the news reached Saul that David had escaped from Keilah, he made no further move" (1 Sam. 23:1–13).

The ascendancy of the prophets in Israel was due, apart from the inspiration of their teaching and the example of their lives, to the need the people had to be told what to do, to be shown the way, to have their choices made for them. The immediate reaction before any doubt was "to consult the seer," the one who sees, the prophet, the saint, the man of God. When the Temple was defiled and the altar profaned in the time of the Maccabees, the priests didn't know what would be the right thing to do with the stones of the altar, and so they took them apart and kept them in a clean place "till a prophet would appear and could declare what had to be done with them." The people are helpless without a prophet. The desolation of Israel, repeated through years of exile and defeat, is above everything else that "there is no prophet" (Ps. 74:9). Without a prophet, Israel doesn't know what to do. Israel wants to know what the ways of the Lord are, and its prophets are the normal channel through which those ways are declared to his people.

The need to know, the desire to be enlightened, the prayer of the Psalms: "Lord, show me your ways." No need is greater, and no grace is more welcome. To know your ways for mankind and for me, for your people's history and for my private options, for the great events and the daily choices. To know what pleases you. To know your mind. To know your will. To know you. I begin to realize that the exercise of finding out your divine will is the highest possible concern of humankind, as knowing your will is knowing you.

In a painful and paradoxical way, the very apostasy of

Israel in the desert was due to the desire (exaggerated, misplaced, unworthy, childish, but still a desire) to have concrete practical gods who would lead the people in a visible and detailed way through the dangers of the desert. The people's request to Aaron said it explicitly while Moses remained absent in the remote search of an unseen God: "Make us gods that will go before us." Make us gods we can see and feel and touch and follow as they open the way for us in the wilderness and lead our battles and show us our land. That is what the golden calf had to be. A concrete guide, a visible god, a palpable leader. Someone to show the way, to lead the march, to "go before us." True, the people of Israel had the guidance of the "cloud" that went before them during the day, and the fire at night. But the cloud was precisely only that, a cloud, too abstract and impersonal and unclear. It could not be grasped, defined, comprehended. Israel wanted a god with a face and a body and a clear program and detailed leadership. And that was its sin. It didn't want the mystery and the darkness and the cloud. It didn't want the uncertainty and the dangers and the delays. It didn't want the long march and the daily risks. It didn't want to have to find its way and to make its choices and to fight its battles. And God was angry with his people, and Moses broke the tablets of the law and melted the golden calf and reduced it to dust and mixed it with water and made the people drink it. The sin had to be expiated. The wrong guidance. The slavish dependence. The abdication of responsibility. That was unworthy of the people of God. We do want guidance, but we want it as God wants it, in mystery and darkness and trial and risk. In seriousness and responsibility. In maturity and courage. In discernment and faith. The cloud that guides while remaining a cloud. And the glory of God resides in it.

There is a standard way, primitive and universal in time and space, which man in his naïveté has used to ascertain

God's will in moments of doubt: to cast lots. And it is instructive to think of what there is behind that seemingly innocent practice. "The lots are cast into the lap, and it is the Lord that orders them" (Ps. 16:33). Right up to the eve of Pentecost, when the Holy Spirit would descend on the nascent Church and would change forever the ways of discernment with his presence, his wisdom, and his guidance, the disciples of Jesus resorted in simple faith to this elementary way of making an election. The matter was important. Judas had gone "where he belonged," and his place in "The Twelve" had to be taken by another among those "who were in our company while we had the Lord Jesus with us." "Two names were put forward: Joseph, who was known as Barsabas, and bore the added name of Justus; and Matthias. Then they prayed and said, 'Thou, Lord, who knowest the hearts of all men, declare which of these two thou hast chosen to receive this office of ministry and apostleship which Judas abandoned to go where he belonged.' They drew lots and the lot fell on Matthias, who was then assigned a place among the twelve apostles" (Acts 1:23–26). Here there must have preceded a previous scrutiny, a discussion, a proposal of names, a list, an obvious exclusion of candidates till only two remained, and these two evenly balanced with no easy choice between them. And then the last step is left directly to God with a prayer.

Once I witnessed very closely the delicate process by which a prospective bridegroom is chosen in an Indian household. The girl in the family has come of age, and her parents let it gently be known among friends and acquaintances and caste-fellows that the prospects are open and suitors are invited. They come. Directly, indirectly, discreetly, openly they come and inquire, show interest or quickly withdraw in a complex web of multiple claims and conflicting choices. I know well, from repeated confidences of marriageable girls, the psychological stages through which the bride-to-be has to pass. When the first prospective candidate announces a polite refusal, the girl panics and goes into a fit of anger, despair, and self-hate. "I'm good for nothing; nobody will want me; nobody will marry me; we should have started earlier; now it's too late, and I'm ugly and dark and short and fat and useless and will have to remain single for life." It is painful to hear a lovely girl talking such nonsense and crying her eyes out in self-pity, but I've endured the ordeal more than once. Then a boy says yes, and the girl's immediate reaction is, "Such an idiot! He thinks he's good enough for me? Has he seen himself in the mirror? He can't even look straight, and he wants me? Fat chance! Let him look elsewhere for another victim. I'm not that cheap." And so the game goes with its ups and downs, and gradually anxiety subsides, serenity sets in, and all at home and even the girl herself begin to see that there are good choices, and each begins to draw up his or her favorite list, and some names get cancelled while others go up, and slowly a consensus emerges in the family, and numbers are given to the names: who is first and second and last. And then the final selection comes. It was so in the case I am writing about. After many days and many interviews and many consultations, the result was similar to the biblical choice of Pentecost eve. Two names stood out, and the girl and the family found it impossible to decide between the two. The girl reported the situation to me and informed me of the solution: "We're going to cast lots between those two, and the lucky one will have me." But what tickled my theological sense of humor was her spontaneous comment on that course of action. "After all," she said with charming resignation, "we have to leave something to God."

I am full of respect for that wonderful girl, as I am for the apostles even before Pentecost; but I want to be free to analyze the attitude of mind that lurks behind the casting of lots, and the religious belief that handles everything by itself till it feels baffled, and then has recourse to God as supreme arbiter in difficult cases. When it was a question of whether the prospective suitor had good looks or not, good health or not, sound finances or not; when it was a question of finding out (really!) how many false teeth he had and whether the squint in his left eye was only in the photograph or a real defect; when it was a question of choosing between a dark or a fair boy, tall or short, rich or poor . . . they didn't cast lots about it. They definitely knew what they wanted, made sure of it by themselves, and took it or left it on their own. They took no chances there. They cast no lots. So long as they could function on their own, they did. Only when they couldn't make up their minds did they resort to lots, consoling themselves with the belief that in doing so they were (however belatedly and reluctantly) leaving the final issue to God. That is the attitude of "the God in the gap," the God that becomes active only when we reach the limit of our faculties, an attitude that is unfortunately common and theologically disastrous in understanding faith and seeking God's will. That is, I'm on my own so long as I can manage, and when my strength or my intellect or my means or my information or my influence can do no more, when I find myself helpless, when the "gap" appears in my life, I rush to God to fill it in, and call that faith and devotion and surrender and acceptance of God's will. I go to the doctor so long as his remedies work, and when he gives me up I turn to God. That is a distorted view of religion, of discernment, and of life, and I want to expose it clearly at the outset. The true view is that my choices (as all my actions) are fully God's and fully mine. God is present in my discernment from the very first moment the quest begins. He presides over my inquiries and accompanies my doubts, he guides my views and assists my decisions. He is there all the time, in my strength and in my weakness, in my search and in my goal, in my anguish and in my deliverance. I live my life in his strength and his grace, and I make my choices, fully and entirely as they are, in his wisdom and his light. He is not a last resource but a constant companion, not an emergency measure but a permanent source, not a God in the gap but a living God in every breath of my life and every event of my existence. To know his will in my choices I have to live it first in all my days.

God is free, though, to use even our imperfect ways to bring about favorable results. I must record, and do so most willingly, that the boy and the girl of the previous story did marry, and their marriage was and remains to this day a very happy one. And St. Matthias, of course, became a worthy apostle. There is comfort for us in God's goodness and his readiness to use even our limitations for his ends. Let us make our choices as best we know—and trust that God will straighten in the end even those we have messed up.

There is also manipulation possible where all these devious ways of choosing are resorted to. A lady who used to come to see me from time to time to discuss her problems, told me one day rather shyly that before coming to me each time she would cast lots to ascertain whether it was God's will that she should come or not. And again she confessed, with further blushing, that when she was very keen on coming and the lots came out against it, she would cast again and again till they came favorable so that she could come with a good conscience. We had a hearty laugh together. And I don't think that stopped her from cheating at the lots. That is often the case with professional diviners: They can accommodate the injunctions of the stars to the client's needs for a consideration. An essential element in every Hindu marriage is the exact fixing of the auspicious day and time at which the ceremony must take place if the happiness of the new couple is not to be jeopardized. Now in a certain African country I visited, there are many Hindus, most of them engaged in trade and business that leave them only Sundays free for social functions and contacts. There are weddings, of course, among them, and astrologers to calculate the auspicious days for the happy events. I received quite a few invitations during my stay there, and I noticed with glee that all weddings took place on Sundays. The stars were ready to oblige.

A problem came up on the day I had to leave that country to come back to India. My air ticket was confirmed, and the departure fixed for the next afternoon. I informed my hosts and started packing. Then I noticed something was happening. My friends were murmuring among themselves, stealing glances at me and looking worried. Finally they came up to me and explained the problem: Not only weddings require an auspicious moment for their celebration, but also any important event, as, in the case at hand, a long journey by air. There are astral moments in which a journey can be undertaken, and moments in which one can in no way start on a journey; and the day and hour of my flight was one of such unfavorable moments.

My friends would not allow me to board the plane under such circumstances, and they let me know categorically their final decision: I could not take that flight. I assured them that personally I was not worried about the position of the stars, and explained to them that: if the airlines had to consult the astrologers for the departure time of their flights, the chaos in our airports would be even worse than that we now suffer. All to no avail. They insisted that "if anything would happen" to me they would feel guilty all their lives for having let me go at an adverse moment, and they asked me to honor their feelings and yield to their request. Before such an approach I was ready to yield; but the airline was not. They did not have another seat till two weeks later, and it was not possible for me to wait till then. Faced with this situation my friends found a clever solution. They asked me to have my luggage and everything ready for the morning of the next day; I would then leave in the morning the house where I had been staying, and I would take leave of everyone as though my journey were starting at that moment. At that time in the morning the stars were favorable and there was nothing to be feared. Then I would just cross the road to the house of another of my friends, as though that was the first stage of my journey; I would stay in that house for the day, and in the afternoon we would proceed to the airport without a care on our souls. My trip had officially begun in the morning, and the curse had been shrewdly avoided. That was the way we did it.

I arrived safely at my destination. I even got the impression that the idea was not new for my friends, and that this was not the first time they were having recourse to the astrological ruse. I learned that with a little bit of good will on the part of all concerned, one can even cheat the threatening stars. After all, one has to travel . . . or to get married, as the case may be.

These innocent manipulations of heavenly data make us smile. But we are all guilty of much more subtle manipulations of the channels of discernment, of creating an accommodating God for our own personal interests, of "bringing God's will to ours" in the standard warning phrase of our classics of the spirit. That is the danger.

And that is my interest in writing this book. A task which is not easy and is important: to sharpen the sense of discernment, the perception of God's will, the respect for his inspirations, the understanding of the dynamics of choices and decisions and elections. Any growth in sensitivity, any deepening of self-understanding, any screening and identifying of our own motives and intentions and inclinations, is progress in life and in grace. The fruit may well be worth the effort.

"Your will be done" is the ultimate prayer that sums up God's glory, the running of creation and the purpose of life. I change the passive impersonal into the personal active concrete voice: "I want to do your will." And to do it I have to know it first. That is my duty, privilege, and prayer. To search in order to know. To know in order to do. To learn to make my daily choices, big and small, new and repeated, difficult and obvious, with increasing faith, understanding, and joy. If my life is my choices, I want my choices to be the best they can be. I want to master the art of choosing.

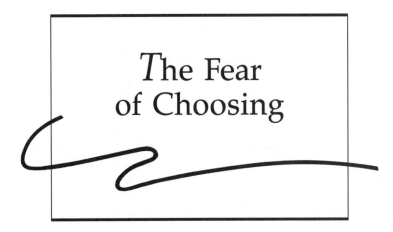

The Fear
of Choosing

Laziness, doubt, and fear are the great enemies of the right choice. I mean hidden enemies. The obvious ones of selfishness and pride and jealousy and greed are also formidable foes, but easier to identify and straighter to fight. The hidden enemies cause more harm because they attack unseen and strike in the dark. They strike at the root. The act of choosing is the noblest and deepest of human acts, the very definition of the person and the expression of the dignity of man. And precisely because it is noble and deep and characteristic of man and constitutive of the person, it is hard and painful and dangerous. That is why our first reaction when faced with a choice is to avoid it, to ignore it, to postpone it. More decisions are made in this world by default—that is by not making any decision and letting things run their course —than by positively and actually coming forward, intervening directly and giving a new turn to events. Volitional laziness is a universal disease.

An exhibition match of a chess master against twenty simultaneous opponents is a feast of decision-making. The twenty boards are arranged along a continuous table, with each opponent sitting in front of his board. The master just walks slowly along the table, pauses briefly before each board, glances at it, muses for an instant, puts out his hand, makes his move, and passes on to the next board. Round after round, move after move. Twenty against one. Total concentration. Absolute mastery. Every move is registered in his mind, every board memorized, every situation analyzed as he moves along without stopping, without hesitating, without delaying. One step, one glance, one move. Another step, another glance, another move. On and on. And every situation is different, every move unique, for each opponent has his own game. The master moves along, his mind ticking out decisions as he moves. In a short span of time he has made literally hundreds of decisions. All in time, definite, exact. And at the end he wins. Most of the games will be his; there will be a couple of draws and an occasional defeat, but in any case the display of art and skill and genius that make up a chess grandmaster. His decisions are only chessboard decisions, but are an image and reflection of what decisions in life can be. Timing, promptness, punctuality in making decisions are also essential to win the game of life.

Another chess situation: In an official match, besides the two players and the referee, there is a clock. An essential witness. It too plays an important role in the game. It measures the maximum time allowed for each move, and the maximum total time allotted to each player. If that time is exceeded, the game is lost. The clock is incorruptible. It ticks away its seconds. It warns, it moves, it strikes. The move has to be made before the hand is up again: The decision has to be taken before it is too late. But the player hesitates. Stretches out his hand and takes it back. Waits. Freezes. Goes blank. Just sits inert. And the clock goes on. The hand goes up. The time limit is over. And the player loses his game. This has happened rarely in the history of world chess, but it happens daily in life. A decision has to be taken. Each decision has its own clockwork, its own time limit, its own measuring device built into itself. And the man hesitates. Doubts, wavers, procrastinates. Just sits idle on life. Extends his hand but doesn't make a move. Thinks again. Whiles his time away. And the clock goes on. Life goes on. The end time for the decision approaches. Comes. Time runs out. The clock strikes. And the game is lost. We could learn for life from a chess tournament: a clock by the side to time decisions and proclaim the penalty for not making them; no decision is always the worst decision; we may lose the game.

My students in college ask innumerable times the question: What is the last date for . . . ? And I tease them: Couldn't you for a change ask, What is the first day for . . . ? They are all last-date addicts. The last date to make a choice, to submit a form, to put in an application. Wait, delay, put off. Don't do today what you can do tomorrow. There is still time, there are many days, nobody has moved yet. Meanwhile the days pass, the calendar slips away, and the deadline springs up suddenly in front of the eyes. Tomorrow is the last date! The magic word. The feared summons. The unavoidable judgment. And then the hurry and the hustle and the haste . . . and the wrong choice. Each decision has its own timing, its own dawn, its own place in the stars, and that has to be sensed, respected, obeyed. Never trespass on the rhythm of life.

We delay decisions because they are hard to make. For the same reason we avoid them, and, whenever possible, try to shift onto someone else the burden of making them.

We are in a group meeting where a decision has to be taken. The matter has been explained, full information has been given, reasons for and against have been exhausted, and finally the chairman asks the straight question: What shall we do then? Notice the silence that follows, the set faces, the downward looks, the awkward stillness of the whole group for agonizing minutes. Nobody wants to be first, nobody wants to define him- or herself, nobody wants to take the risk to come out in the open with a clear personal choice. After one or two have spoken it will be easier to support someone, to agree with him or her, to see the general trend and join the consensus if one emerges, or even to oppose an opinion and side with someone else and maintain a divergent view. We find it easier to function with a prop, with someone or something to lean on, to support or to oppose; with company, with help. The naked personal, direct, independent choice is hard to make and hard to express. A choice commits a person. And we don't commit ourselves easily.

This story made the rounds of religious houses, though its actual source was never accurately established. A religious superior had tried several houses for one of his subjects whose peculiar character made it difficult for him to stay long at any one house. Finally, tired of shifting him around, he called him and told him: "Here is the map of our province and all our houses in it. You choose any one you want, and I'll send you there." To which the restless subject answered with a malicious wink: "That is what I'll never do. I'll never tell you I want to be sent to a particular house. Because if I do, then, when I get tired and want to change, you'll rightly tell me: You yourself chose this house, so now stay in it. And I'll have no answer to that. That's why I'll never tell you where I want to go, so that I always remain free to protest."

No wonder the superior (and everybody else) had trouble with that man. There was certainly logic in his reasoning, as there was unfortunately tortuosity in his attitude. Don't commit yourself, don't choose, don't say where you want to go, leave yourself free and keep on jumping about from house to house to your heart's content and to everybody's annoyance. Refusal to commit himself, to define himself, to pledge himself—that is, refusal to be himself: Make my choices for me means live my life for me—that may be comfortable, but it is cowardly and mean and unworthy of a person. He might have been proud of his stratagem, but deep down he was thoroughly dissatisfied with himself: dissatisfaction which he projected onto each group and each house where he lived, so that he had to leave it in disgust, which was ultimately disgust with himself. He was paying dearly for his refusal to be himself.

Fear to commit oneself. A young man was in the process of choosing a bride (that is, of having a bride chosen for him by his parents), and I asked him with innate Western prejudice, "Why don't you make your own choice and pick your own girl?" And his answer revealed to me an aspect of the complex question of matchmaking I had not thought about. He said categorically, "Never. Let my parents do the choice. That way, if my marriage ever ends in failure I can always blame them." I hasten to say that not all young men think that way about arranged marriages, and the question is delicate and involved, and has a thousand aspects and intricate outcomes. I only take this example here to bring to light and stress a fundamental aspect of decision-making, of its importance, dignity, and radical influence in life. It is this: By making a personal choice I commit myself, take on for myself a direct responsibility, and in consequence will do my conscious, subconscious, and unconscious best to make my choice work so that it proves me right. If the young man marries the girl of his choice, he may, and most probably will in any case, sooner or later have problems with her and difficulties in his marriage; but since the girl was his choice he will try, apart from countless other considerations of children and family and society and religion and upbringing and the good of all concerned, to see his marriage through and make it a success. When I make a choice, I instinctively want to show that my choice was the right one, and therefore I do all I can to make it work. Engaging my personal responsibility in a definite choice brings out the best of my resources and of my very self to meet the challenge and win the day. If I avoid choices and shirk responsibility, I shrink and wither and die. To live a full life I want to be faced with dilemmas, to come to where the ways part, to risk choices, to shoulder responsibility. That makes me come alive, use my resources to the full, and be myself. I want to have no excuses for my failures and no escapes for my mistakes—which is precisely the way to minimize my failures and cut down my mistakes. I want to make my own choices and live my own life for better or worse, it is the only one I can truly live.

Another abdication of responsibility is to leave the decision to the circumstances. This is more common than we imagine. Here is a case: A person is hesitating about whether to go on a trip or not to go. Yes, no. To go, not to go. Doubts, delays, advice, persuasions. Reasons for, reasons against. Desire to go, laziness to remain. Friends invite, family dissuades. Waits, sees, thinks. Finally he inquires. Contacts the travel agency. They tell him the quota has been filled up and there is no place now. And he heaves a sigh of relief: Great! It's fixed now. There is no place. The decision is made for me. No reasons to be given and no explanations to be made. There is no place. Thank God. Thank the travel agency. No place. No trip. No decision. No anxiety. Remain quietly at home, and if anybody says anything, quote the travel agent. Relief. Relax: Circumstances have spoken. Would that others always made my choices for me. It would be so much simpler! Yes, and so much poorer.

Another universal reason to avoid having to make choices, and, when that is not possible, to delay them as much as possible, is the simple but hard fact that when choosing one thing we must give up another. We all claim to understand at once the bit about not being able to eat the cake and have it at the same time; but then in practice we try to negotiate a fifty-fifty deal, and keep at least half a cake

The Fear of Choosing

while we eat the other half—with the problem coming up again about that remaining half. We say confidently "first things first," but we don't realize that that inevitably implies "last things last" and therefore "some things never." That is painful to say. Yet the meaning of both expressions is in the last analysis the same. The essence of choice is precisely to leave out something. The word "decision" comes from *decidere* which in Latin means "to cut off." Decision is surgery, and that makes it painful—though salutary. However pleasant the prospect of getting something, we dislike having to give up all the other choices equally possible till then; and in an effort to soften the farewell we delay the parting.

I watched a small girl go through the painful decision of choosing between two dolls in a shop full of toys. Her mother had told her plainly: one or the other; you choose. Now, disjunction does not come easily to children. They understand readily "both" or "none," but not "either or." And that linguistic difficulty may well be effect and reflection of the reluctance to choose, the refusal to have to leave out something in order to take something else. The little girl acted out the "both" by packing one doll under each arm and showing with conviction that she could well walk away with both; and when her mother resolutely stopped her she enacted the "none" by leaving both abruptly and strutting away in a dignified huff. When her mother stopped her again and explained patiently that one doll was better than no doll, the child finally understood and picked out one of the two. The doll was packed, paid for, delivered, firmly secured by the girl's tight grip. She looked once more to the doll that was left behind, and I fancied I saw guilt and remorse in that look of the innocent child for abandoning the other doll. Then her mother took her by the hand, and was leading her out of the shop when she did something unexpected and beautiful. She broke loose, rushed back, went to the place where the rejected doll had been left, gave it a kiss and ran again to her mother. In that kiss was all the pain and the regret and the helplessness and the agony of the choice that could not be. A lovely child was beginning to learn how painful it is to choose.

The Mixture Within Us

Early in my spiritual life I read Faber's classic *Growth in Holiness*. For me it was then reading the right book at the right time, and its impact on me was deep and long-lasting. The following thought, if not the words, was in that book and has remained with me since: Not a single action, even by the greatest of saints, is ever performed out of pure love of God. Maybe it was my own reluctance to believe it that made me remember it. Surely the saints were exemplary, and at least some of their actions pure as gold. Yet a master of the spiritual life was warning me that there is more to human behavior than meets the eye. Later in life I heard about mixed motives. I studied their reality and discovered their pervasiveness. The master was right. Every choice is tainted.

I think of selfless sacrifices, of heroic service to fellow humans, of ascetical hardships and consecrated silence, of virginity and martyrdom; I think of long prayers and contemplation and self-denial and humble obedience; and I think, of course, of all the thousand actions done daily by good men and women in simple faith and honest living as they order their lives the best way they can in their genuine desire to do good and please God. Acts of love, of service, of virtue, of religion. And on each of them the shadow of a lower motive. I don't in any way want to diminish even by a hairsbreadth the value and the merit and the beauty of any noble act done by a generous heart. But I do want to know the workings of that heart and the limitations of the human condition. I want to know and accept the fact that my motives in acting are mixed. And I want to know the mixture.

It is easy to see the mixture in others. The politician who stands for an election because he wants to serve the people. One of R.K. Lakshman's unfailing cartoons depicted members of the routed opposition party debating among themselves over what to do next, with worried faces, and the pointed caption: "Let's change over soon to the ruling party; else we'll lose our chance to serve the people." Maybe by dint of repeating the slogan they themselves come to believe it. No one else does. A candidate for governor in the state of Missouri was more honest when he declared: "There isn't any great public outcry for me to do this. I just want the office."

I want to transcribe here a testimony as a positive witness to this situation, and as a tribute to a revered friend and outstanding statesman, the late Chimanbhai Chakubhai Shah of Bombay. His words: "I have the habit of analyzing my motives in whatever I do, much as a scientist analyzes a chemical substance, to find out what is beneath my external behavior and bring to light the real motives of my actions. People may believe that I do something out of an ideal of service to the people or to the country, and the reality may be quite another. I give an example. I was a government solicitor. When the 'Quit India' movement started, I immediately went and handed over my resignation. I became a hero overnight. My patriotism, loyalty, sense of detachment and sacrifice for the country were praised by one and all. My resignation from such an important post was hailed as a major achievement in the struggle for Indian independence. Yet the reality was quite different, and I knew it. I was just happy and relieved to be able to get out of that job. I had accepted it only under pressure by Kher and Munshi, and with a pay of only six hundred rupees. I was longing to resign, and when I saw the chance and did it, I felt as though I had been liberated from jail. People praised me, but I knew my own story. It is this type of self-examination that I prize."

And well he might. Such serenity to see the real motive, and honesty to manifest it, are rare. The real motive. The actual cause. The hidden impulse. Why did I do what I did? I've written in another book (*I Am Collecting Rainbows,* the chapter entitled "I Am My Feelings") that by asking "why" I never get to the real reason. "Why" goes to the head, and motives are much more complex than pure thought. They are reason and feeling and past and present and tradition and prejudice and influences and reactions and hopes and fears and everything on earth mixed up and baked together. Each motive is like one of those radicals in chemistry with chains of hexagons and links, and radii jutting out and capital letters written at each corner to mystify the layman and enlighten the initiate. Or, more sweetly, each motive is a piece of puff pastry. What the French call *"Feuilleté,"* and the Spaniards *"milhojas."* A thousand sheets, leaves, layers, flakes, and in between them jam and cream and chocolate and jelly. A thousand tastes in one bite. Defying all definition. Defeating all analysis. It takes a very good confectioner to make crisp puff pastry—and a good gourmet to appreciate it.

A psychology textbook lists the following primary motives of human actions: safety, love, pleasure, money, fame, power, and religion. All lists are naive, and each item can be eternally subdivided into further lists. All entries overlap and no enumeration is exhaustive. And apart from the abstract list of primary ingredients, my point is that in each concrete choice, in each real action, all those elements and their derivatives mix and combine and interplay and interact in ways ever different and each time unique. The thousand tastes. The individual pastry. The single choice.

Why did I become a Jesuit? Again the "why." Let me try the "how" and "when" and in which way and under what circumstances. All that can cast light on a fundamental choice in my life, made in my youth, nursed through my growing years, maintained against crises and treasured to this day in humble recognition and joyful gratitude. When I joined at the tender age of fifteen, and for many years after that, when the question was asked: Why did you join? I answered always willingly, spontaneously, almost aggressively: Because God was calling me, and I was sure of it; as sure as I am that you are now standing in front of me and talking to me. The experience had been so clear and so strong for me that I was ready and happy at any moment to bear witness and repeat my story, and indeed I have set it down in print in my Gujarati autobiography with definite clarity and candid faith. My vocation for the religious life has always been for me a personal example of how God can make his own voice heard in the hearts of human beings with absolute authority and total exclusion of any doubt. If I had not joined, I would have felt guilty and considered myself a traitor for the rest of my life. And the underlying feeling was one of personal love for Christ. I was not joining in order to do great things or work for others or save souls, but simply and directly to love Jesus without obstacle or distraction, with all my heart and for all my life. That is how I felt then, and in writing this after so many years I am only trying to reflect my original feeling as exactly and faithfully as I consciously can.

It is only recently, when repeated contacts with human nature have made me grow wiser (is it truly wiser?), that I have noticed a shadow over that outstanding memory of my life, and have had the courage to allow myself to look into it. I have simply examined the external circumstances prevailing around me at the time I took that transcendental step in my life. And this is what emerged: I had lost my father only a few years before, and after that had lost also my family home and all possessions in the ensuing Spanish civil war. We were left with only the clothes we had on. My mother had had to borrow money, learn a trade, go to work as a typist, place us in a boarding school where my brother and I obtained scholarships, while she lived with relatives and managed to eke out a living for the three of us. Our financial future was by no means bright at the time. And then another circumstance: I was in a Jesuit school and boarding, and the prevailing atmosphere at the time was that the best students unfailingly joined the novitiate. The cream, the elite, the top of each graduating class went every year straight from school to cloister. It was a privilege, a tradition, a matter of prestige. The best boys joined. And I was top of my class. Those were the years of postwar Spain when there was a great revival of faith with the consequent revaluing of the priesthood and religious life, and bumper crops of vocations year after year. And the Society of Jesus was then at the height of its prestige and influence in that climate of religious fervor. To become a Jesuit was an honor and a privilege, and a family that had a son in the Society improved its social standing. In that atmosphere and in that school one almost needed courage those days *not* to join the novitiate. It would have been at least awkward for me not to toe the line. And yet another circumstance: There was pressure brought upon me, subtle but direct pressure. In one incident I was praying alone in the school chapel when the Spiritual Father, whose main concern was to ensure that all prospective candidates would keep the pledge, approached me stealthily from behind and said in my ear with an underworld tone of voice: "Hear the voice of Christ from the cross, who commands you to follow him into the novitiate." I knew all right that it was not an angel that had spoken to me, as I had recognized well enough the voice in spite of its hollow tone; but I was also young and pious and gullible, and the unworthy trick did have its effect on me and confirmed my choice. These are the shadows I find. There was pressure on me; to join was a matter of prestige; and by joining I eliminated financial worries and the struggle to have to come up in a competitive world. Three solid points.

Let me set things down clearly. I am not in any way saying that my vocation was not valid, that I was tricked into joining, that I regret it or that I was a mere toy in the hands of circumstances. I am not saying that. God works through circumstances, and he can even work through the hollowed voice of a well-meaning and ill-acting Spiritual Father. I have no quarrel with things as they are and with history as it has happened. No complaints and no regrets. On the contrary, confirmation and joy and thanksgiving. What I do say is that those elements too were part of my choice, and I didn't know it then nor for many years after that. My motives were mixed, even in that holiest of my life's actions, and I never so much as suspected it. There was the element of prestige and safety and pressure where I thought there was only pure love of God and a heavenly call above all suspicion. My choice stands, and in a way I sense it more firmly because I now know better how I made it— shadows and all.

Why did I come to India? Again, I've told the history of the "why" in the book I mentioned earlier. As a follow-up of my commitment to Christ, an intimate Jesuit friend talked me into applying for the foreign missions in order to give up my country as I had given up my family, and live only for God. Again a most worthy choice. And again, now, the shadows. That was the moment in my career when my personal professional future had to be decided. Within the Society of Jesus I could be many things, and I had no clear idea which. I just didn't know which line would be best for me, and my Provincial, who had to decide, didn't know it either. He had asked me to propose what I wanted to be, and I didn't know what to say. The most promising student in the class didn't know what to do with himself. An embarrassing situation. And the sudden proposal of my zealous friend had shown me a splendid solution in the nick of time. The missions. No wonder his persuasive words had an immediate effect on me. I had no missionary zeal at all, but I had now something to propose to my Provincial, an honorable and intelligent choice when all eyes were on me and rumors had begun to spread about my future. The sudden announcement of my appointment to India burst on the house like a bombshell. I suddenly became the center of attention, and all kinds of praise, admiration, holy envy, and hero worship were lavished on me. In a farewell speech someone said of me that I was another Grandmaison and another Teilhard. Amusing, of course, but none the less gratifying for me to hear. To go to the foreign missions in those days of ardent faith and apostolic revival was a heroic deed, a noble endeavor, the supreme sacrifice. I basked in the sunshine. I had found a brilliant solution to the thorny problem of my future. I could be proud of my choice. I flew to India.

Curiously enough, and for the very first time in my life after so many years and so many remembrances of that friend whom I have thanked countless times in private letters and even in public talks and in print for having been providentially instrumental in my missionary vocation—curiously, I say, and unexpectedly, as I am writing this now and remembering him. I feel for the very first time a clear resentment against him. Again, not regret that I came to India. I'm happy here. But resentment because he manipulated me. With the best intention in the world, of course, with his zeal and his faith and his love and his dedication (he himself went as a missionary to another end of the world), but he had lured me, pushed me, imposed on me, prevailed upon me. His was the idea, the proposal, the insistence, the pressure. Left to myself I would have never so much as thought of it. It was his doing. It was his choice, not mine. And together with the affection I've always professed for him and my appreciation of his own worth and his care for me, I'm now allowing myself for the first time in my life to feel this resentment for his intrusion in my life-decision, or rather resentment against myself for having allowed him to rule my life. It is not the end result that concerns me here, but the way that led to it. I am happy about the outcome—and critical of the procedure. It was an important choice in my life, and it was not mine.

Those two choices had occurred in my youth, which was a rather inexperienced and immature youth, as I was shielded from contacts, isolated from society, anonymously enrolled in a group of like-minded people who did what they were told to do, and thought what they were told to think. I don't say that as an excuse to defend the weakness of my choices, but as a circumstance that partly explains it. The trouble is that, as I say that, I'm reminded now of another important decision in my life, far from my youth and well into ripe adult age, and I fear that this one is not going to stand analysis either. And yet I don't feel reluctant to go into it, but, on the contrary, eager to learn from my past whatever it may bring. I turn the searchlight on again.

About twelve years ago I made the decision, and obtained all the legal permissions for it, to go to live with poor Hindu families in my city (Ahmedabad), begging hospitality from house to house, sharing their life in everything, and coming daily on my bicycle to teach in the college from eleven to five as any professor who comes from outside. That way of life was new, unusual, out of community, risky, and hard. I told my superiors and companions that God was clearly calling me to that kind of life, as I had clearly discerned under much grace in a charismatic retreat I had made, and I asked them for their prayers and their blessing. They promised both—while they could barely hide their misgivings. I had only informed them that that was God's will for me; I didn't consult them, didn't ask their opinion, didn't even make a show of taking them into confidence in making my choice. Bad policy. They were good enough not to oppose my decision, but they resented it. In fact my relationship with my group wasn't at the highest at the time. I sensed friction, uneasiness, tensions. And turning my searchlight on the dark spot, I see now what I stoutly refused to see then; namely that in putting up this scheme of going to live outside, I was conveniently escaping from the tensions of living at home with my group. Not that I was consciously doing it for that reason; my religious motivation, my desire to live with the poor and share their life was genuine, and this manner of life (I lived in that way for ten years, and came back to my community only two years ago) has been an immensely fruitful period of mental and spiritual (not physical!) gains which I treasure and value in grateful memory. But there was a dark side to my decision, and it had fully escaped me at the time.

And still one more side. Those were the days when work with the poor was coming to the fore all around, and whoever wanted to be something among us, had to distinguish himself on that front. So far my work of teaching higher mathematics in college, and of writing books and articles, was rather an elitist (the damnable word now) kind of occupation. Now here was my chance to qualify, to outdo the champions of the poor, to get into fashion, to graduate from the field itself into the ranks of the new breed. I did it. It turned out fine. But in doing so I was satisfying a hidden need of mine which was not mentioned in the charismatic manifesto of my inspired discernment.

And more. With my Hindu friends, with my readers and my public in India, this new bold venture of mine also brought me redoubled recognition and praise and applause. They appreciated my gesture, they publicized my wanderings, they glorified my stand. I had by then written many books and given many talks, and this new experience gave me the chance to say something new, to gain fresh attention, to renew the limelight. I notice with alarm that the prestige motif has come up clearly and powerfully in each of the three important choices of my life that I've analyzed. Pretty disturbing. I mean, what is disturbing is the fact that I hadn't noticed it. And then, into the bargain, the experience of those years gave me matter for three original books. Frill benefits. And none of them budgeted for.

Why am I writing this book? Why do I write at all? One thing is definite, though unorthodox: I don't write to do good to others. Well-wishers kindly tell me: This book of yours will do much good. Fine if it does. But I know I'm not writing for that. I like it much more when someone tells me: I really had a good time reading your book. Never mind whether it does him or her "good" or not. I am wary of moral judgments. If someone truly enjoys the book and lets me know it, I feel happy. I do write for self-expression. The joy, the urge, the tide, the organic need to think and express and write and publish is undeniable, and I experience it to the full. The Indian *rishis* carved their thoughts on the bark of trees in their solitary forests. Their impulse surges in me too. Readers or no readers, I want to write, and my publishers kindly keep up the necessary supply of bark (doesn't paper come from trees?) so that I *can* write. I also write as an occupation, as a profession, as a means to have an answer ready to the unavoidable question, What are you? A writer. I do know the story of the Jesuit intellectual who was asked by one of his younger brothers, "What do you do for a living?" And he serenely answered, "I think." I haven't yet reached that exalted state, and still want an earthly title on my visiting card. And with the occupation goes therapy. Occupational therapy. Writing fills my days and oils my brains and calms my soul. The writing of this book is actually a poignant example. Some days ago a somber calamity fell on my family and affected my mother, and me through her. (Maybe some day I'll write about it. Now the wound is too fresh and will bleed if I touch it.) For a few days I was numb with sorrow, and my pen lay idle. I knew there would be balm in it, and yet refused to touch it. I delayed my first contact with it morbidly, almost masochistically. I didn't want to be distracted from my pain. Finally I took it up and began this book. The pain continues, but is now gently bearable. Writing is medicine. The fact is my spirits have soared again, and I feel fine indeed. Life goes on. And writing goes on.

I also write because I want recognition. After bringing to light the role that prestige and fame have played in important choices in my life, I cannot very well ignore that. And I know it is true. I like to get good reviews of my books, I like my name to be known, I like to get literary prizes and to be talked about. I want my books to be read and liked . . . and bought! I know when I'm writing good stuff, and I privately enjoy in secret anticipation the pleased comments of imagined readers. Recognition gives me satisfaction.

There is one more motive in this complex web of my literary activities, this time a more respectable one. I am referring now to my English publications, this book with two others that have preceded it and a number of others that are lining up in my mind, ready to follow. For years I had written only in Gujarati for a largely Hindu readership. I had always stoutly refused, though the suggestion was often made to me, to write books in English. (Again, why did I refuse? I used to tell others and myself that my consecration to Gujarat demanded of me to write only in Gujarati. Beautiful reason. Today I know I didn't write in English because I was afraid I would fail. Another mixture for the collection.) Finally I took the step, and I am sharply conscious of the main reason that led me to take it. I noticed that while happily working with and among Hindus, I had somehow distanced myself from my Jesuit companions. In particular the ten years I spent living from house to house in Hindu neighborhoods, while giving me an invaluable experience of closeness and identification with the people, had weakened considerably my links with my own community, and through it with the whole religious body of Jesuits to which I belong. Few Jesuits read my Gujarati books. I then thought that if I wrote in English on the religious life, I could strengthen my links with my own brothers. That would bring me reactions, mail, discussions, disagreements, and in any case the renewed contact I wanted. That consideration influenced my choice. I started to write in English to strengthen my Jesuit roots. It was a happy decision.

This leads me to the last point I want to make on mixed motives: how they help or hinder dealing with others and with common life. In fact mixed motives, when suspected and not manifested, are an obstacle to true relationship. I listen to my brother explaining in the group his work, his plans, his choices. I externally praise his motives, which are all spiritual and pastoral and ascetic. I commend his dedication, his humility, his self-sacrifice; I support his proposals and endorse his plans. Meanwhile, inwardly I judge him to be acting out of desire for power, security, and prestige. And in his absence everybody else says the same about him and his apostolate. Contact is nonexistent. And the same happens when I present my own work and my own projects with their official motives . . . and without the true ones. I do get a green light—to nowhere. Communication has not taken place. Frustration increases. That is the painful story of some community meetings, though it may not be reflected in the minutes.

Mixed motives. To know them myself, to manifest them when required. A hard program. A necessary endeavor. Transparency. Honesty. Truth. Important for the person and important for the group. The way to grow. The path to perfection.

I'm sure that if I ask my group companions to comment on what I've written here, on why I do the things I do and behave the way I behave, which they know only too well, they will certainly have some fresh motives to add to my list. And I honestly would like to know them—complimentary or not. I want to know why and how I make my choices. I realize that it is a complex task, and all help is welcome. I know I'll never cease.

This has been a hard chapter to write. As I come to the end of it I realize it's quite a disturbing one too.

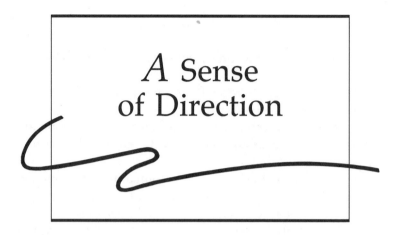

A Sense of Direction

My central idea in planning this book was to comment on St. Ignatius' ways to make choices and find God's will. It's time I get down to that more directly—though all I've said so far has also been part of my Ignatian makeup in one way or another.

"To order one's life," "to seek and find the divine will in the disposition of one's life" is how Ignatius words the aim of his "Spiritual Exercises." For him that was the supreme question of man's life on earth. He found himself at thirty with his life in his hands, uplifted by an experience that urged him to the highest deeds he could conceive; generous and ambitious, yet hesitant and doubtful as he didn't know the new ways and had no one who could enlighten him in the early days of his new life. He wanted to know God's will for him, to know it in the concrete, and to know it with certainty. He suffered much in the process. He had to learn by experience. Sometimes he fasted to know God's will, he was easy prey to doubts and even felt temptations to suicide. As he advanced and matured and grew more attuned and sensitive and experienced, he came to feel that God was teaching him "as a schoolmaster teaches a pupil." He turned out to be a good student, and eventually an accomplished master himself in the art of discernment, the art of "ordering one's life."

If the whole Spiritual Exercises are a treatise on how to put order in one's life, there is still a treatise within a treatise in the compact guide on how to make an "election" that Ignatius inserts in the middle of his text. His first principle in it is that "the eye of our intention has to be simple," which is only a direct translation of Jesus' saying in the Sermon on the Mount, "If your eyes are sound, you will have light for your whole body; if the eyes are bad, your whole body will be in darkness. If then the only light you have is darkness, the darkness is doubly dark." To have light, to see, to distinguish and enjoy line and color and nature and life, to discern the ways of the spirit, the path to the heights . . . we need clear eyesight, a healthy eye, an unimpaired vision, a straight view. Singleness of purpose, clarity of mind, definiteness of intention. To know what I want, to aim at it, to do it. The map, the goal, the compass. And then no compromise, no hesitation, no wavering. A definite course and a single-minded resolution to follow it. That is the first requisite of a good choice. Once the aim is clear, the means will become clear too. Without a definite aim there can be no intelligent choice of means. Without a "single eye" there can be no bull's-eye.

Ignatius had a lovely little habit of his own. He would stop himself bodily in the middle of a corridor and ask himself in his own mind: Where am I going and what for? I'm going to the chapel to pray. I'm going to the dining room to eat. I'm going out to meet somebody. Where and what for. Every moment. Every step. Almost the Zen practice of knowing what I do, being where I am, eating when eating, and walking when walking. With the Ignatian twist of the aim, the purpose, the direction. Where am I going? What

37

for? Give me the map. Check my bearings. Fix my course.
Each checking on my course is done in function of the ultimate aim of my whole existence. Each "where am I going?"
is a reminder, a reference, an actualizing in a small concrete
step of the overall purpose of my life. By ordering my steps
one by one, I order my life. By knowing what I want to do
with my life I readily come to know what I have to do with
each step.

Ignatius explains the "simple eye": "Looking only at
what I've been created for, that is, the praise of God our Lord
and the salvation of my soul . . . ; our first object has to be
the service of God, which is our aim . . . ; and so nothing
should move me to take up or leave something except the
service and praise of God our Lord and the eternal salvation
of my soul." When giving talks on this matter I revel in
Ignatius' text and enjoy producing quotation after quotation
(which is quite easy, having placed between the pages of the
book careful markings in advance) to hammer in Ignatius'
monotonous repetitiousness and almost boring insistence on
his one obsession: the service of God and the salvation of my
soul. I also realize now that what works very effectively in
speech does not do so in writing, and to give now a string of
repetitious quotations would be the best way to stop the
flow of the book and kill its momentum. And the point is
clear by itself without the repeated quotations, namely that
a right choice needs a basic aim, a sense of values, a world-
view, a frame of reference within which it is to be made and
fixed and followed. Students of mathematics know that in
geometry often a "change of axes" can solve a problem—or
create one. Perspective is important.

When Air India's first jumbo jet "Emperor Ashoka"
nose-dived into the sea off Bombay after take-off, killing all
aboard, the main cause of the accident turned out to be the
malfunctioning of the "artificial horizon," a device that gives
the pilot with pictorial clarity and constant accuracy the an-

gle that the aircraft's wings make with the horizon at any one time. The pilot had taken a turn after the initial lift, but the artificial horizon had failed to register it. Thinking, then, his wings to be still horizontal, the pilot took a further turn —which added to the unregistered one proved too much and ended the life of the plane and of all in it. That device is essential for a safe course and a happy landing. The horizon, the balance, the angle. Any failure in its functioning may cause an accident. And plane accidents are measured in lives.

What is it that makes the horizon turn and signal a wrong angle and cause a crash? Ignatius has a name for it: "inordinate attachments." So long as the horizon floats freely in view, unhindered, untrammeled, the course is straight, and the turns, when required, are taken in safety. But if the device clogs, sticks, adheres, any turn can be deadly, and every choice is vitiated at the root. That is the attachment, the imbalance, the blurred sight. Ignatius has a simpler comparison: the weighted scales. For the scales to measure the exact weight, they have to be delicately balanced. Any deviation in their structure will give the wrong weight.

When I was learning the piano in my youth I was so fanatic about it that once, when the only available instrument was an old piano, every single key of which was out of tune, I kept practicing at it for hours on end each day, disregarding entirely the sounds that came out of it, and concentrating only on speed in reading and accuracy in fingering. It was only after many days that the services of a professional piano tuner could be secured, and after a whole day's labor he set the instrument right. When I then sat at it and began playing my daily assignments, I felt as though the gates of heaven and all its angelic melodies had burst open suddenly before me. That was music, melody, art. What I had been doing before was only finger technique and speed reading and wrist work. Sheer bodily drudgery. Now here was the reward of perseverance and dedication. The exact melody, the perfect chords, the complete composition. I continued to practice, but now I liked what I heard and enjoyed what I played. I myself wondered how I could have put up for so long with a piano so out of tune. What tuning is to a musical instrument, clarity of purpose is to life. It is essential to produce music. Without it one can practice, but miss the music. And in that experience of mine I see a figure of what a life out of tune can be: toiling at the keyboard, and no melody in the ears. Confusion of values, blurred principles, and cloudy ideals can, like loose strings in a piano, turn an otherwise meritorious life into a joyless experience. Much noise and no music. Remove the disturbing "attachments." Call the tuner soon.

The effect of the attachments is to distort the image, to blur the vision, to alter the order of things. They make an end out of the means, and a means out of the end. The means before the end. The cart before the horse. The order of life upset. I've given many examples throughout my life to convince myself and others how foolishly we often act in our lives by placing a passing whim before a lasting concern; but recently the daily newspaper brought me a twentieth-century example of an ancient truth. The buses that ply long distances from Surat to Bombay, Nasik, and Ahmedabad, had been recently fitted with videos that constituted a new attraction, and a welcome entertainment to passengers in the long hours of the tedious journeys. Then the papers reported the case of the passenger who bought his ticket at the Surat bus-stand to go to Bombay, but on boarding his bus and inquiring of the conductor which film was to be shown during the trip, found it not to his liking, while he also learned that the bus for Nasik would be showing a picture he was keen on seeing. He acted fast: changed his ticket, changed his bus, and went to Nasik instead of going to Bombay. He had no business in Nasik, and he missed his Bombay work, whatever it was. In compensation he saw a picture he wanted to see—which he could in any case have done more comfortably on a video at home without traveling to Nasik. But the sudden desire altered the order of things. The main became subsidiary, and the subsidiary main. Going to Bombay was the end, and seeing a film on the way was only a very very secondary consideration in the long journey. But the focus was changed. The artificial horizon malfunctioned. The scales tilted the wrong way. The impulsive attachment interchanged values. The film became the end, and the bus journey only a means to that end. So he swapped buses and landed in Nasik. The newspapers did not say which other city he went to from Nasik the following day. Possibly he returned to Surat in order to see his favorite picture once more in the same bus.

Where am I going and what for? That little question, opportunely repeated, can undo much mischief in life.

A closer look at things. The attachments can be hidden and can be obvious. And I don't just mean here that those of others are obvious while our own are hidden, but rather, and more subtly, that our own attachments are at times apparent to ourselves, and sometimes quite hidden from our sight. There lurks danger. I may have a weakness for chocolate, and indulge in it when I get a chance; and I am the first to know it and to realize that it sometimes makes me depart from the ideal diet I should be following for the good of my body and the perfection of my soul. I can get heartburn, and I know my nemesis. But chocolate alone is not likely to make me stray from my life goal. Not only because the attachment is small, but because it is obvious. Much worse is the disguised attraction, the persistent weakness, the hidden preference that draws the mind secretly and effectively to unhealthy choices under cover of innocent tastes. I'll never cease uncovering plots in my mind and treason in my heart, and each time I examine past choices I find new depths and new darkness in the secret recesses of my soul where decisions are taken and life is made. I'll never cease knowing myself.

Here is a prayer from the "Exercises," in fact from the first consideration of the first week, condition, and basis of further progress and advancement in the ways of the spirit. "To ask Our Lady to obtain for me from her Son and Lord the grace to feel the disorder of my actions, so that holding it in abhorrence, I may mend my ways and order my life." For me to achieve order in my life I must first feel and sense and experience the disorder within me. Essential grace.

The Blight
of Compromise

Man is a political animal. And the essence of politics is compromise. Yes and no. Yours and mine. Both and neither. Don't commit yourself, or you'll lose votes. Vague answers, general promises, all-embracing statements. Try to please everybody, or at least not to positively displease anybody. The joint communiqué, the vigorous handshake, the smile for the cameras. Give the impression that you are everybody's candidate, and be ready to strike an electoral pact with any party if that can assure victory at the polls. Pacts, understandings, compromise. Give up something and get something in return. Squeeze through. At any expense. That is politics.

That is life. That is practicality. I don't want to give up my "attachments" even when I've found them out, and I resort to the tactics of the politician. Compromise. Yes and no. Give and keep. Of course, I'll do my duty. But I'll hold back something. I'll be generous with God, and, taking refuge in that very generosity of mine, I'll find an excuse in it to keep for myself something that God won't mind very much in any case, and that I definitely want for myself. There is a

blunt saying in Spanish: Hold one candle to God, and one to
the devil. The candle for God will, so I understand, be bigger
and better and richer than the one for the devil, as one has to
keep the proper order, and to respect rank and seniority; but
there will be another candle anyhow before that other altar
—that is, before my own selfishness and greed and pride.
And I will justify the smaller private candle with the wider
glamour of the bigger one. To hold back, to bargain, to compromise. That is the opposite of the clean choice, the full
determination, the commitment. That is unworthy of a person.

St. Paul has a magnificent passage which I love, where he
vehemently condemns compromise, double dealings, hesita-
tions, and false promises. He had been accused of precisely
that by his enemies (whom he definitely had); and that vex-
ing calumny drew from him a spirited reply that moved from
vigorous self-defense to high theology, and upward to one
of the most imaginative, deep, and spontaneous definitions
ever given of Christ as the Yes and the Amen, which is the
clarity in asserting, the firmness in proclaiming, the joy in
living to the full the word and the promises of God. "I had
intended to come first of all to you. That was my intention.
Did I lightly change my mind? Or do I, when I frame my
plans, frame them as a worldly man might, so that it should
rest with me to say 'yes' and 'yes,' or 'no' and 'no'? As God is
true, the language in which we address you is not an ambig-
uous blend of Yes and No. The Son of God, Christ Jesus,
proclaimed among you by us (by Silvanus and Timothy, I
mean, as well as myself), was never a blend of Yes and No.
With him it was, and is, Yes. He is the Yes pronounced upon
God's promises, every one of them. That is why, when we
give glory to God, it is through Christ Jesus that we say
'Amen' " (2 Cor. 1:15–21).

Yes and No. G. K. Chesterton, in a humorous and philosophical mood, mused once on how convenient it would be if the English language had a word between YES and NO. He proposed the hybrid "YO." Here is a proposal: Do you want it, yes or no? Well . . . wait . . . yes . . . no . . . "YO"! The perfect answer. The neat escape. I don't say no, and so I don't hurt anybody, and I don't say yes, and so I don't commit myself. Mathematical logicians propose now multivalued logics with one or more truth values between yes and no. The common person had anticipated the mathematicians' discovery by centuries. The art of compromise far preceded the art of modern logic.

Ignatius exposes the same game by speaking of three types of people with three types of answers to an intimation of their conscience to give up something that prevents them from "finding God in peace." The YES, the NO, and the YES . . . BUT NOT NOW. A clear acceptance, a plain refusal, and . . . a convenient delay. That is only a face-saving device to say no, to keep the attachment while apparently preserving a good relationship and giving a polite answer. But the harm is done. In fact the in-between answer causes more harm than a clear refusal, because the refusal creates awareness of opposition, rebellion, and withdrawal, which may in its day generate repentance and reconciliation; while the measured postponement refuses cooperation but keeps up appearances and dulls the edge of conscience. The master of compromise has managed to keep his "attachment"—to his own undoing. This Ignatian consideration is called "the heart of the election" by an insightful commentator (Iparaguirre).

God wants a clean choice. To keep back something from what he asks, to delay, to compromise is to hinder rather effectively his action in the soul. A choice, even in the right direction—if it is incomplete, if it leaves out something, if it tries to cover up what it keeps back with what it gives—is not a genuine choice. It can do great harm.

The Art of Choosing

To make a good choice, make it clean.

To make a good choice, make it full.

To make a good choice, make it definite.

Half measures will never do.

Sometimes we wonder, and we have full right to wonder in humility and faith, why things don't work, why our prayer does not take flight, why sacrifices do not bear fruit, why years of renunciation remain barren. Far are God's ways from our limited understanding, yet it is also open to us to examine and question and guess. And masters of the spirit point out this pervasive cause as a common villain. Half-heartedness, half-measures, partial surrender—which is no surrender. Lukewarmness which is neither hot nor cold, holding back, playing games, divided loyalties—which again are not loyalties. No wonder things don't work when they are not what they are meant to be. How is it that our children drink milk and don't grow fat on it? asks a Hindu preacher. And he answers: Because the milk they drink is not milk. Then he adds: The religion we in practice profess is no religion. No wonder it doesn't work. Pointed indictment of many a spiritual life.

Bonhoeffer, who chose the beautiful and serious title *The Cost of Discipleship* for his central book, said in it: "Is there some part of your life which you are refusing to surrender before God, some sinful passion, maybe, or some animosity, some hope, perhaps your ambition or your reason? If so, you must not be surprised that you have not received the Holy Spirit, that prayer is difficult, or that your request for faith remains unanswered. Go rather and be reconciled with your brother, renounce the sin which holds you fast—and then you will recover your faith! If you dismiss the word of God's command, you will not receive his word of grace. How can you hope to enter into communion with him when at some point in your life you are running away from him? The man who disobeys cannot believe, for only he who obeys can believe. No one should be surprised at the difficulty of faith, if there is some part of his life where he is consciously resisting or disobeying the commandment of Jesus."

It is a law of nature that water at sea level and free from impurities, boils at a hundred degrees centigrade. Or rather, that is the definition man has given of a hundred degrees of heat. Now, we heat water up to ninety-nine degrees, and complain that it hasn't boiled. After all our effort, the fuel, the heat, the ninety-nine degrees . . . and no boiling! Isn't that unfair! Is not our effort appreciated? Does all we have done count for nothing? Are rules so rigid? Is nature so insensitive? We are hurt and offended and angry. And, of course, we would be much wiser to save ourselves the irritation, and take the little trouble to add one log more to our fuel, one degree more to our heat. And the water will boil.

As a teacher I've had the unpleasant task of correcting examination papers in mathematics through many years. Rules are strict, and marking fairly exact. There is a little margin, personal impression, grace marks; but when all sources are added together, if the grade is thirty-two in a paper of one hundred, the student fails—by one point, as the statutory minimum is thirty-three. And when the student knows his result and his grade, his protests echo loud down the corridors of the college. Failed by one point! Is there any justice? Have those professors any sense? Couldn't they give me just one point more? For one single point I have to repeat one full year! There is no proportion, no appreciation of all I've done, no justice! And, of course, no way out. It's too late and rules are rules. Again he would have been better advised to add to his effort in order to add to his result the one point that in the end would have made all the difference. One single point can ruin a career.

And now, there is a law in grace, enacted by the Lord and

giver of all grace himself: "Nobody can be my disciple unless he gives up all he possesses" (Luke 14:33). True, this is not a blind rule or a mathematical percentage, perhaps not even an external requirement in actual forgoing; but it is clearly an attitude, an expectation, a commitment. And the word is "all." Not "half," not "two-thirds," not "90 percent." All. Else you cannot be my disciple. If in attitude and disposition and surrender you renege and keep something back, you cannot come. Compromise invalidates discipleship.

One clarification. The "attachment" that can play so much havoc is not a passing weakness, an occasional short-coming, a temporal failure. We all are full of those. A thousand faults are compatible with a genuine good will, and are no hindrance to real progress and advancement. The harm comes form the permanent attachment, the twisted will, the ingrained viciousness. It is not the occasional tripping up that interferes with the course, but the wrong direction. It is there that any deviation has to be sought, found, and corrected if we want to reach the goal. Human weakness is no obstacle; it is only willful obstinacy that can rob us of the prize. And here comes our prayer: Lord, you have given us the grace to make the big sacrifices; give us now the grace to make the small ones.

St. John of the Cross insists on this doctrine with firmness and clarity. He takes thirteen chapters to explain the first verse of the first stanza of his first mystical poem—that is, the line "Upon a darksome night"; and the eleventh of those chapters is devoted entirely to this essential theme. In it he says: "Any imperfection to which the soul is attached and addicted is a greater hindrance to advance and grow in perfection than many daily independent faults which don't proceed from a fixed habit or a set condition. Whoever has such an attachment can well give up any idea of advancing in perfection, be the attachment ever so small. What do I care whether the thread that keeps a bird tied down is thin or thick! So long as it doesn't break it, it won't fly. It's true that a thin thread is easier to break, but, however easy it may be, so long as it doesn't snap it, the bird won't fly. And so it is with the soul. Whatever its virtue may be, so long as it is tied down by a willful attachment, it will not attain the freedom of divine union."

And now he gives a famous illustration. Those were days of discovery voyages, when courage and adventure launched man on a sea of whose currents and winds and calms he knew still very little. In the need to explain the strange stillness to which a vessel was sometimes subject in the high seas, they had resource to a small fish, the "remora" or "suckerfish," which attaches itself to bigger fishes or to ships by means of a sucking disk on top of its head, and which, so they believed, rendered them stationary at sea. John of the Cross, who writes from the monasteries of inland Castille, sees in the story he had heard from seagoing adventurers an image of the situation he wants to describe: "This attachment and addiction works in the soul as they say the remora works in a vessel on the high seas. It is a very small fish, but if it happens to stick to a ship, it holds it so quiet and motionless that it doesn't allow it to sail nor to reach harbour. And so it is a great pity to see some souls, like rich vessels loaded with gold and good works and prayers and virtues and graces that God gives them, who, lacking the determination to put an end to an attachment, a whim, a disorder—which is all the same thing—cease to advance and never reach the harbour of perfection. They had only to remove that little sticking fish, to take wing and break the thread of attachment; but they don't. It is a great tragedy that, having had God make them break thick heavy ropes of sin and vanity, they now miss their goal for not giving up a childish attachment which God wanted them to overcome, and which is only a thread and a hair. As a piece of wood will not become fire so long as one degree of the required heat be missing, so the soul will not see itself transformed into God so long as such a stain remains."

John appeals then to Scripture, with the deep spiritual sense to read into situations of the people of God the lessons and warnings for our own pilgrimage. The story is told in the book of Joshua, and the lesson John draws from it is strong and clear. Israel had laid siege to Jericho. The Lord said to Joshua: "Look, I have delivered Jericho and her king into your hands." Israel, on its part, to recognize God's hand in the attack and thank him, undertook to proclaim a "ban"— that is, to take a pledge that they would not profit themselves in any way or keep for themselves any booty, but that everything in the marked city would be burnt, destroyed, and killed, except valuable vessels that would be saved for the cult of the Lord. That was a way, however crude, to proclaim their gratitude and their loyalty to the Lord who gave them victories on the way to the Promised Land. These were Joshua's words: "The Lord has given you the city. The city shall be under solemn ban: everything in it belongs to the Lord. And you must beware of coveting anything that is forbidden under the ban; you must take none of it for yourselves; this would put the Israelite camp itself under the ban and bring trouble on it. All the silver and gold, all the vessels of copper and iron, shall be holy; they belong to the Lord and they must go into the Lord's treasury" (Jos. 6:17–19). The plan worked. Jericho fell, though it was a well-defended bastion, the Israelites rejoiced, and the city was laid waste.

"But the Israelites defied the ban: Achan son of Carmi, son of Zabdi, son of Zerah, of the tribe of Judah, took some of the forbidden things, and the Lord was angry with the Israelites" (7:1). Joshua knew nothing, however, about Achan's misdeed and the Lord's anger, and planned new exploits ahead. Next on the map was the city of Ai, near Bethaven, east of Bethel. He sent spies to reconnoiter, and they reported that the city was small and easily accessible, so there was no need to send the bulk of the army; two or three thousand soldiers would be more than enough for a quick job. Three thousand were sent . . . and were thoroughly routed by the men of Ai. Thirty-six were killed, the rest chased down the valley, and Israel was left to mourn its dead, to smart at its defeat, and to wonder what had gone wrong with its men who could conquer an impregnable fortress like Jericho and were put to flight by a smaller group in an open place. "At this the courage of the people melted and flowed away like water." Was the Lord no longer with them? And why?

"Joshua and the elders of Israel rent their clothes and flung themselves face downwards to the ground; they lay before the Ark of the Lord till evening and threw dust on their heads. Joshua said, 'Alas, O Lord God, why did you bring this people across the Jordan only to hand us over to the Amorites to be destroyed? If only we had been content to settle on the other side of the Jordan! I entreat you, O Lord; what can I say, now that Israel has been routed by the enemy? When the Canaanites and all the natives of the country hear of this, they will come swarming around us and wipe us off the face of the earth. What will you do then for the honor of your great name?' The Lord said to Joshua, 'Stand up; why lie prostrate on your face? Israel has sinned: they have broken the covenant which I laid upon them, by taking forbidden things for themselves. They have stolen them, and concealed it by mingling them with their own possessions. That is why the Israelites cannot stand against their enemies: they are put to flight because they have brought themselves under the ban. Unless they destroy every single thing among them that is forbidden under the ban, I will be with them no longer. Stand up; you must hallow the people; tell them they must hallow themselves for tomorrow. Tell them, these are the works of the Lord the God of Israel: You have forbidden things among you, Israel; you cannot stand against your enemies until you have rid your-selves of them' " (7:6–13).

The procedure to find out the culprit was rather involved, and included casting lots as well as making direct and indi-rect inquiries. Finally Achan was discovered, and he con-fessed: "Achan answered Joshua, 'I confess, I have sinned against the Lord the God of Israel. This is what I did: among the booty I caught sight of a fine mantle from Shinar, two hundred shekels of silver, and a bar of gold weighing fifty shekels. I coveted them and I took them. You will find them hidden in the ground inside my tent, with the silver under-neath.' So Joshua sent messengers, who ran to the tent, and there was the stuff hidden in the tent with the silver under-neath. They took the things from the tent, brought them to Joshua and the Israelites, and spread them out before the Lord" (20–23). The Lord was given his due. And Achan, with his sons and daughters and oxen and asses and sheep, saw done unto him what he was to have done to the riches of Jericho. And "the pile of stones remains to this day." The next day Israel attacked Ai and conquered it.

John of the Cross comments: "This was done so that we may understand that, to enter into the divine union, every-thing in the soul has to die, much or little, big or small, and the soul has to remain without any greed, free and untram-melled, as though all those things were not for her, nor she for them." The allegory fits neatly. The promised land to-ward which we are making our pilgrimage and for which we are fighting our battles is the Kingdom, salvation, contem-plation, freedom and justice and purity. God's ban is the injunction not to draw the line anywhere, not to keep any-thing back, not to do things by halves, not to compromise, not to cheat. Then come the attachments: the two hundred shekels, the Shinar mantle, the bar of gold. Each one has his own list, his peculiar weaknesses, his pet attachments. Gold and silver, or even just a mantle. Anything will do. Anything that breaks the ban, spoils the whole, mars the relationship. And then the worry and the anxiety and the complaint. Why is it we don't succeed? Why don't we advance, why don't we experience grace, why don't we break free? Our efforts don't bear fruit, our best work leaves the world untouched, the Kingdom is farther than ever, and our own lives languish in dull routine. Where are the hopes, the victories, the Promised Land? A small enemy routs us, any vulgar temptation lays us low. Our lives never quite flower into grace and wisdom and joy as we were told and we had hoped they would. Where is the Spirit and the power and the resurrection? Where are God's promises and the assurances of the gospels and the witness of the saints? Where do we stand, if we stand at all in this dreary life and this desert land? . . . God has an answer. Simple and plain. Clear and definite. The pact has been broken. The ban has been defied. The condition has not been kept. Something is missing. Awake and examine and purify and surrender. Search the camp and find the tent. The two hundred shekels and the Shinar mantle and the bar of gold. Dig them out and give them up. Then you will see victory.

In case the Shinar mantle looks a little remote from our experience, here is a closer case. A devoted and hard-working religious had little by little built up for himself a filing cabinet with notes and references and sketches and quotations for sermons and talks and writings and meditations, neatly arranged in equal cards with tabulated indexes, cross-references, and flip-card titles jutting out for instant fingering. A fine tool of work for a minister of the word. In the process of building it up, however, he had grown so much attached to it that when, at the end of his studies, he had to go to make a thirty-day closed retreat that was part of his formation, he feared God would ask him to sacrifice that pet possession and give it to someone else; he worried about the future of the treasure he had so carefully and lovingly put together through the years. Then he found a way out. Before entering into retreat he went to a trusted companion, handed over to him the filing cabinet, and told him, "I'm going for a thirty-day retreat. Keep this thing for me here safely. Now listen carefully: Whatever I tell you during these thirty days, don't give the cabinet back to me. Keep it yourself. It is safer in your hands. You never know which queer mood I may get in, and I wouldn't like to do in the heat of fervor something which I'll later regret. So keep it yourself. And when I come out after the month, when I come back to my senses and to sanity and reliability, then, yes, do give it back to me and I can use it safely the rest of my life." Clever plot. But it misfired. The man went into retreat and tried to pray. There were meditations and contemplations on sin and death and the life of Christ and his passion and resurrection. But all the meditations of this man had only one single object: the filing cabinet. Do I keep it, do I leave it? He didn't get out of that. Not for the whole month. It was an obsession, a nightmare, a plague. He couldn't forget it, couldn't put it aside, could not go ahead, could not think, could not pray. Only cabinet—no cabinet. Do I keep it?—Do I give it up? I can inform my friend, but he is instructed to disregard any message. And, anyhow, how am I sure God really wants me to give it up? Let me continue peacefully with my retreat, and I'll see at the end. But he had no peace and no retreat. Nothing would work. No prayer, no contemplation, no devotion. Only the accursed object and the distracted soul. And now I have to leave this story incomplete because I don't know its end and I don't want to invent it. Maybe the kind director told him to keep his cabinet; maybe he burnt it; maybe his friend played him false and refused to return it and kept it for his own use. All possible ends to the story. But one thing I know: the filing cabinet, however legitimate and harmless and useful, effectively ruined the thirty-day retreat of that zealous priest. A single "attachment" can ruin thirty days of prayer—and a whole life of spiritual endeavor.

This insistence on total openness with God and on the negative consequences of the lack of it is no exaggeration, and certainly no divine whim or outdated understanding of a fearful God who exacts payment to the last farthing from his helpless subjects. On the contrary, it is, going deeper into the meaning and the mystery, the true-faith understanding of God's own nature. It is God's holiness that is at stake, and that is what makes the matter serious and urgent. God will bear no conditions and will not lower himself to any bargain. He is a holy God. He is patient and merciful and understanding, and will forgive all transgressions and forget all faults; but he wants a true heart and a sincere will. There he stands no compromise. He is a jealous lover. He will not share our heart with anyone, with anything. The attachment for its own sake to something that is not he, vitiates at the root our relationship with God and makes it impossible for it to grow and fill our lives and give us satisfaction. God will not share his throne with any creature. The priests of Dagon at Ashdod had a rather explicit experience of this. "After the Philistines had captured the Ark of God, they brought it from Eben-ezer to Ashdod; and there they carried it into the temple of Dagon and set it beside Dagon himself. When the people of Ashdod rose next morning, there was Dagon fallen face downwards before the Ark of the Lord; so they took him and put him back in his place. Next morning when they rose, Dagon had again fallen face downwards before the Ark of the Lord, with his head and his two hands lying broken off beside his platform; only Dagon's body remained on it. This is why from that day to this the priests of Dagon and all who enter the temple of Dagon at Ashdod do not set foot upon Dagon's platform. Then they sent the Ark of God on to Ekron" (1 Sam. 5:1–5).

The Hebrews had many types of offerings with their

rules and customs and rubrics. The supreme sacrifice was the holocaust, and as such it is described first in the ritual of Leviticus. The word says its meaning: "holocaust" is Greek for "whole-burnt." In it the offering, which was a bull or a ram or a goat, had to be burnt, and burnt fully after the ritual killing at the altar. No portion of it could be kept for the priest or for the offerer. It was fully dedicated to the Lord, and therefore fully destroyed. The people of Israel knew that, and so did its priests and ministers, but not all kept the sacredness of the whole-offering. And God proclaimed his wrath through the prophets: "I hate cheating in the holocaust!" Give it to me or don't give it to me. That is up to you. But if you do give it to me, give it fully. I don't want your bulls and your goats in themselves. They are not my food. But I want your will and your heart, and if your heart is not whole in your offering, it is no use to me. You have other sacrifices where the priest keeps one part and the offerer receives back a share. Use them freely when you want your share. But the holocaust is fully for me. And I don't stand cheating. God has his self-respect too.

The Lord speaks through his prophet Malachi: "A son honors his father, and a slave goes in fear of his master. If I am a father, where is the honor due to me? If I am a master, where is the fear due to me? So says the Lord of Hosts to you, you priests who despise my name. You ask, 'How have we despised your name?' Because you have offered defiled food on my altar. You ask, 'How have we defiled you?' Because you have thought that the table of the Lord may be despised, that if you offer a blind victim, there is nothing wrong, and if you offer a victim lame or diseased, there is nothing wrong. If you brought such a gift to the governor, would he receive you or show you favor? says the Lord of Hosts. But now, if you placate God, he may show you mercy; if you do this, will he withhold his favor from you? So the Lord of Hosts has spoken. Far better that one of you should close the great door altogether, so that the light might not fall thus all in vain upon my altar! I have no pleasure in you, says the Lord of Hosts; I will accept no offering from you. A curse on the cheat who pays his vows by sacrificing a damaged victim to the Lord, though he has a sound ram in his flock! I am a great king, says the Lord of Hosts, and my name is held in awe among the nations" (Mal. 1:6–14). The holiness of God presides over his dealings with his people. That is why compromise has no place in the life of the spirit. The Lord is holy.

More on Compromise

The danger inherent in compromise, in half measures, in leaving something, however little, out of the whole, is a theme that seems to haunt man's imagination, as it is found in myths and legends of distant literatures all over the world. Achilles' body was rendered invulnerable when immersed in the waters of the Styx—but the heel by which his mother Thetis held him during the operation remained untouched by the powerful waters and thus open to wounds in war, and to Paris' arrow that found its target and killed him through the unlikely aim. In a very similar way Siegfried's bath in the dragon's blood converts his skin into an armor—except for the spot on his back where a leaf had fallen and stuck during the bath, and where Hagen's spear lands to send him to his death. And then the Indian version in the Mahabharata: Duryodhana knew that his mother, Queen Gandhari, had the power to render him impervious to any weapon. She had acquired the power to grant that boon by the strange penance that marked her life. Her husband, King Dhritarashtra, was blind, and she, in sympathy and submission, had blindfolded herself for life to identify with her blind husband.

That exalted merit had conferred on her the power to render invulnerable, if she removed her blindfold, the first person on whom her sight would fall, by the hidden energy accumulated in her eyes during their heroic penance. Her son, bound for the battlefront, thought he was the obvious person to benefit from his mother's merit, and so he approached her, first removing all his clothes so that the protecting sight would fall directly on his whole body and render it immune to blows and wounds. But there too an accident occurred. (An accident is necessary to ensure that man remains mortal, and that epics can be written.) The house gardener saw him going naked into his mother's presence, and threw a garland of flowers around his waist to embellish him and to protect his modesty. He went in, Queen Gandhari removed her blind, the blessing descended on her son's body—except for the belt of flowers. And it was there again that after many exploits in the battlefield Bhima's mace descended, found its mark, and ended Duryodhana's life. Man in all climates seems obsessed by the thought that something, however little, if left out of the whole, can spoil the final effect and render useless the best efforts and the surest schemes. A flower, a leaf, a thumb holding a heel—and a hero's life is lost and a legend is born.

Apart from literature and theology, this attitude of mistrusting the incomplete choice and the halfhearted decision is just good common sense and sound psychology. To hold something back weakens the commitment and impairs determination. To leave a loophole, an escape, an alternative, undermines willpower and fosters retreat. I am not at my best when I know I have a second option, a possible retreat; I think that if the first course of action doesn't work, I can always fall back on the second, and that prevents me from going wholeheartedly for the first. The total commitment brings out the best in me; the cowardly compromise does no justice to myself.

The Art of Choosing

I once got into trouble with an article of mine in the Gujarati press. Well, more than once, but that time more particularly—and not unexpectedly. Many Indians have sons and daughters settled abroad, and some resented the trend of my article, which concerned them. In it I gave two real cases I knew. In one of them an Indian, who had been many years with his family in America, decided to come back and settle in India for the rest of his life. He was not sure, however, whether he could get a satisfactory job here, and so he took only a three-month leave from his job in America, kept his house and car and everything there, and came to India to look for a job. He did look and found something, but was not satisfied. The three months passed quickly, and he declared, "I'm really sorry. I did mean to come back and settle here for a number of reasons, and I've made an honest effort to do so; but my effort has failed, and, very reluctantly, I have to go back to the States." And he did. The other case was similar in appearance, but different in procedure: Another Indian also settled in America with his family, and also determined to come back for similar reasons. But he acted differently. He resigned from his American job, sold his house and his car and all that could be sold, packed the rest of his belongings and came to India with his family. He also had to look for a job, and did not find it in three months. But he could not go back. He told me later that in those difficult months he had thought endless times, "If I hadn't resigned my job and sold my house, I would definitely go back to America at once." But he had cut off the way to go back. He had committed himself. He had to go ahead. And ahead he did go. And eventually he found a good job. And then a better one. And he succeeded. And his family was happily resettled in India. And he blessed his determination, and congratulated himself for it.

That was the article. And the bag of mail it brought was heavy. Heavy with letters and with abuse. My son earns so many dollars a week there, and where is he going to get anything near that here? I sacrificed all my earnings to send my son abroad, and do you want him to come back and settle to a dull existence like mine? If my son leaves his job there and doesn't find one here, are you going to pay for him and his family here? Pretty spirited, that one. Reactions like that make me feel a writer's job is not so bad after all. If an inconsequential article in the Sunday paper can stir a reader to write a sharp retort like that, there must definitely be something in writing. Those letters brought out the fighter in me, and I followed up my article with another one the following Sunday to clinch the job.

That article was the story of Shivaji and Sinhgadh, dear to every Indian boy and to every lover of Indian history. Sinhgadh means "The Fort of the Lion", and Shivaji sent his best general, Tanaji, to conquer it from Aurangzeb in his own freedom struggle. The fort was taken, but Tanaji was killed in the battle, and the news of the victory and the death prompted the famous exclamation from Shivaji's lips: "I've got the Fort, but I've lost the Lion." Now, how the fort was taken was the point of my story. The stratagem is also famous in Maratha history. Suryaji carried out the attack under Tanaji's orders. He tied a rope to a giant iguana that climbed the rampart, held fast at the top and allowed a young boy to climb through it. Once up, he secured a rope ladder at the top, and Tanaji's soldiers climbed through it in the dark. When all had climbed, Suryaji took out his sword and cut the rope ladder. That left his soldiers only one way to go. Strike ahead and fight Aurangzeb's men. Win or die. There was no way back. There was no ladder to climb down. No escape. No retreat. And the soldiers were brave anyhow. They fought and they won. A ladder had helped them to climb, and the same ladder, courageously cut by their leader, had helped them not to think of going back. That is the way to victory.

I like that attitude. I love that determination. I personally hate compromise. It doesn't go with me, with my character, with my way of doing things; it doesn't fit, it is not me. If I want to do something, I do it, and if not, I leave it; but if I do it, I do it in full. I go the whole hog. To the bitter end. No half way. No weak measures. No fifty-fifty. Cut your ladder and burn your boats. Don't leave loopholes. If you leave them, you're sure to use them. Ladders are to climb up, not to climb down. But if left hanging on the rampart, someone will remember it and use it in flight. And others after him. And the battle will turn out different, and history be written another way.

To commit myself brings out my resources, increases my faith, and steadies my course. To keep outlets for failures is not to have faith in myself, not to have faith in God. And to be weak in faith is to walk lame through life. Faith does not hesitate, and expresses its heavenly reassurance in its total irrevocable commitment. I believe . . . but not quite, means simply that I don't believe. Faith does not come in portions like cream cheese. Neither does life. Take it or leave it. And if you take it, take it full. It is all of a piece.

I don't know how to bargain. I am utterly helpless in a flea market where no item has a price tag, and where the final payment of every piece of merchandise is the end result of a long battle of wits between the hardened seller sworn to his or her profit, and the prospective buyer ready to fight inch by inch the unknown price of the doubtful exhibit. I suffer every time I get down from a motor rickshaw in my beloved city of Ahmedabad, and I ask the driver how much is the fare, and he just smiles at me, and I point at the meter, and he says it doesn't work, and I ask again, and he smiles again, and I insist, and he says I can give him whatever I want, and I say I'll give him the just fare, and he obsequiously defers: "Your good pleasure, sahib," and I say I have no good pleasure, and he says: "What your heart tells you to give," and I say that my heart is telling me to give him a kick in the pants and go away, but he doesn't believe it and smiles some more, and I do want to pay him his due, but I don't know whether it is five rupees or twenty or maybe fifty, I'm totally ignorant of these matters, and I'll make a fool of myself whatever I give him, and I'm ready to give him a good tip if only he tells me the exact fare, but that he'll never do, and I tell him about the tip, but he sticks to his oath, and he is all patient, and I'm all impatient, and I give him something, and he first makes as if not to take it, but then laughs himself and touches the money to his forehead in ritual acceptance, and goes away contented in his accursed rickshaw, and I swear I'll never get into a rickshaw again, and I feel miserable, cheated, insulted, humiliated, frustrated, and exhausted. O rickshaw drivers of my beloved city! If bargaining is an art, you are its masters! But I'll walk, and I do choose to walk my legs out, but for impossible distances, rather than fall a prey to your unholy ways. Bargaining be damned! I prefer a fixed-price shop to all the bargains in the world.

"We spend many years, sometimes a whole life, keeping back something, bargaining with God whether we should give ourselves entirely to him or not." These are words of a great spiritual master, Fr. Lallemant, and they are the story of our lives too. Bargaining, hesitation, delay. Delays are bargaining too. Haggling with time. Today, tomorrow, later. Augustine's prayer: "Make me chaste . . . but not now!" Make me holy, make me pure, make me detached, by all means, Lord, purify me and sanctify me and mend my ways and redeem my life . . . only not right now, please! Right now I'm too busy, I'm doing many things and enjoying them, and I'm young and I have a whole life ahead of me in which I definitely mean to serve you and love you with all my heart as nobody has done yet, and I'll certainly do it and I pray to you from now to help me do it, and I know you'll do it and the day will come and I'll be yours and my life will be different and I'll be happy and pure and committed to you wholly as I truly want to be and dream that I shall be. Beautiful dream. And idle prayer. True, God, in his mercy, heard the first part of Augustine's prayer and ignored the second; but when I look around and see that there are not many Augustines, I fear that God does not always do that. A bargain prayer is a lame prayer. A compromise deal is unworthy of God and unworthy of man. That is not the way to the heights.

Someone has spoken of waiting-room addicts. And that is the worst addiction in life. The waiting rooms of the spirit, the antechambers of the palace of the soul are full of people who are just there, and stay there, and pitch their tent there, and live there and die there. The fact that they are already in the waiting room gives them the sense of being on the move. They've already left home, they have reached the station, they have a ticket, they are definitely going places. But not yet. For the time being they have settled in the waiting room —and they wait there. And the trains come and go, there is movement all around, and crowds and noise, and the whole of mankind is going everywhere at the same time, and engines whistle and coolies shout and children weep and humanity sweats, while the ceiling fans in the waiting room of the Indian railway station move slowly, slowly, slowly over the man who has made a pillow of his suitcase and sleeps on it on the floor as permanent tenant of the halfway house whom nobody will disturb because he is going nowhere. The convenience of waiting saves the anonymous guest from the perplexity of arriving.

Which is again the reason why we prefer to wait. Somebody has said (and I honestly don't remember who): The problem is not to walk, but what to do when we arrive. The problem is arriving. To walk is easy, because it is delay and in-between and distracting and amusing. So long as we walk, we don't think and don't worry, and are entertained by the trees and the clouds and the birds and the sky. But to arrive forces the decision, and that is unpleasant. What to do now? Walking is just a disguised way of waiting. More dignified than being the unofficial guest of the waiting room, but just as insidious. Keep walking so that you may not be faced with decisions upon arrival. And in our lives walking is activity, busyness, hurry, endless occupations and constant work. Everything that protects us from thinking and shields us from decisions. Keep walking so that you may not have to think. Keep busy so that you may not have to face yourself and your life and your decisions. Wait. Delay. Deflect. If you are going to reach somewhere, start again. Go round and round, work more and more so as to postpone decisions and avoid commitment. Man is lazy by nature, and laziness of the will is greater than laziness of the mind: reluctance to make decisions is even greater than reluctance to work. Hence the delay. Put off decisions so as not to have to make them—which is the worst decision.

In my visit to the Roman catacombs years ago I detected a waiting-room syndrome whose memory has remained vividly with me down to the very words of the Latin inscription. I save the scholarship and quote only the two telling words: *"audienti protractae."* That is: "to the listener who overdid her time." Here "listener" means "catechumen," a girl who was "listening" to a course of instructions to be baptized. But she delayed baptism. That was not an unusual practice at the time. Precisely because of the realization of the importance and responsibility of baptism, of the new life it entailed and the new obligations it imposed, of its social consequences and its religious commitment, some people delayed the great day, the change in their lives, the final decision. This girl apparently did so. She delayed the date, she protracted her listening—and she died waiting. An accident, a stroke, a sudden death. We don't know. The inscription gives no details. But she died without the waters. And she was no martyr either; no baptism of blood. Only the procrastinated intention and the deferred action. Her devoted teacher *("patronus fidelis"* in the inscription) recorded the fact with love and regret. The blessing of peace, *"In Pace,"* which accompanies the tombs of Christians is not inscribed by her side. She died in the waiting room. Most of us do.

John of the Cross, at the end of those thirteen chapters I made reference to, sums up his decisive doctrine on the evils of compromise—and, poet that he is, does it in verse. This time, however, it is not the five-verse stanza called "lyre" in Spanish, which he carried to its all-time perfection in his mystical poems with the purity of his concepts, the tenderness of his metaphors, and the exactness of his rhymes. Rather, it is a homely doggerel that he uses to make his point and leave it sticky and stubborn in the memory of the reader, its very comic primitiveness guaranteeing its permanence in the mind. I've never tried my hand at verse of any kind, and this occasion gives me the chance to fill that lacuna in my life with some confidence by putting into English the mystic's nursery rhymes. They'll sound awful in any case, but I can reassure my readers that they are not much worse than the original, which doesn't even scan properly and lacks consonance, maybe to reflect precisely, in its very literary poverty, the spiritual nakedness it proclaims. Its point is that "anything" at all, if taken by itself apart from God, will effectively block our way to God:

> If ever at something you stop,
> you will fall short of the top;
> if at anything you nod,
> you have no treasure in God.

Bad enough, but neat and direct. The message is clear, and the doggerel hits home to its target. If you stop at something, you miss the whole. Remember it and act up to it. The terms are uncomfortably clear, and the challenge steep. There is no other way to "Mount Carmel" whose ascent John describes. He even draws maps of the climb with "nothing, nothing, nothing" on the paths that reach the "all, all, all" at the top. He was no mean cartographer.

The definitive condemnation of compromise comes from Jesus himself in one of his clearest and strongest and most personal pronouncements: "No one can serve two masters. Either he will hate the first and love the second, or he will follow the first and despise the second." And he applies his saying to money: "You cannot serve God and Money." Curiously, Ignatius does the same in the consideration that has prompted these pages on compromise. He speaks there of money. Money is indeed the prime example, the tangible parable, the symbol of power, the instrument of pleasure, the supreme "attachment" to signify and represent all the other material and spiritual, rough and subtle, thick and thin, obvious and hidden attachments that bind our soul and weigh down our spirit and stop our progress. You just cannot serve two masters. Choose and decide. You can't have both. You can't have me and something else. Cut through and go ahead. Else you'll stick and wait and linger and stay, and eventually get nowhere. Don't delay. Don't hesitate. Ban compromise from your life if you want to make the right choices and obtain freedom and reach me. That is the way—because I am the way.

The Worst
of Advisers

Sometimes I have to draw a line, I mean physically to draw a
straight line on paper, not "to draw the line" which is again
a decision and an attitude; I'm not referring to that just now
here, though the whole book is on that. I'm just thinking of
an example of what I want to deal with in this chapter, and I
say that sometimes I have to draw a straight line on paper to
underline something or to make squares or to mark a margin,
and then I use a ruler. I have an old ruler with me to which
I'm greatly attached: no, this is not one more example of
"inordinate attachment" and its consequences; God knows I
have many such, but this one is of another kind. This one is
just an old ruler which my father used in his work (he was
an engineer and had to draw often), and which is the only
earthly possession of his that has come down to me. It must
have been straight and accurate in his days and in Spain's
dry climate, but in the heat and humidity of the Indian monsoon it warps hopelessly and it is even hard at times to keep
it plane on the sheet of paper. When that happens, I do one
thing. I take it in my hands and give it several vigorous
bends in the opposite direction of the warp. It works. For a

while at least it recovers its neutrality and I can draw straight.

Simple enough. And practical enough. Both to draw lines and to make decisions. To make sure that when I draw a line (or "draw the line"), the line is straight and neat and of the exact length. If I am inclined one way, let me bend over to the other. A little flexing will do good to the muscles of the mind. And the choice will come out straight.

We all are warped. There is a regular monsoon in the metereology of our souls which seeps and bends and spoils and twists beyond recognition the delicate machinery where our choices are made and our lives are ordered. And we know it. We know that we are inclined to some things and averse to others, that we are partial, attracted, attached. The ruler is warped. Take it in your hands and give it a good solid twist in the opposite direction. Then draw the line.

That is exactly the note Ignatius appends to his consideration on compromise. He centers it again on money, and says: "One thing to note: when we feel ourselves drawn away from actual poverty, not neutral between riches and poverty, it is a great help, in order to end with that inordinate affection, to ask in prayer, even against the flesh, that our Lord may call us to actual poverty, and that we want it, ask for it and request it, if only it be for the service and praise of the Divine Goodness." He refers again and again to that note by concrete reference along the whole process of election in the Exercises, and then uses the same tactics in many other contexts.

He even has a name for it: "the other end of the diameter," and that is how he wants us to react when we feel attracted to something base. When we feel ourselves drifting toward the circumference, we must forcibly push ourselves to the other end of the diameter so as to regain the center of the circle. Some cases follow.

On prayer: "When someone feels devotion it is easy for

him to spend the whole set hour in prayer. Yet, when he feels dry, to complete the hour is very hard. To overcome such dryness the man at prayer should stay at it some added time beyond the hour. That is the way, not only to defeat the Enemy, but to overthrow him." This sounds almost like the captain in Ignatius speaking. The best defense is the attack.

On trials: "It is very convenient to react manfully against any interior trial, lengthening our prayers, contemplation, and examination of conscience, and increasing the amount of penance in any convenient way." Do more penance when you feel like doing less.

On food: "To remove all disorder (note the favorite word coming now in the 'Rules to *order* oneself in the matter of food'), it is a very great help that after eating, when he does not feel hungry, the person should determine the amount he should eat at the next meal. Once the amount is fixed, no hunger and no temptation should make him go beyond it; on the contrary, in order the better to overcome every inordinate attachment and temptation from the Enemy, if he feels tempted to eat more, let him eat less." Good dieting help.

Temptation does not stand a chance. If it pulls one way, we go the other. If it wants us to shorten, we lengthen; and if it tries to make us increase something, we diminish it. That is defeating its own purpose. The idea behind it could well be that the Enemy responsible for the attack will realize that he is getting exactly the opposite of what he wants. More prayer and less food. And he may give up the scheme till he can think of a better one.

The great Indian thinker Kalelkar, constant companion and influential adviser to Mahatma Gandhi, once told me himself the following anecdote of his life, which will illustrate the point I am making here. One day in the early morning he went to greet Gandhi as on any other day, but, unlike any other day, he found him sad and depressed. He asked him what was wrong, and Gandhi answered, "You know well that the last thing I do every day before going to bed is to say my prayers, and I never miss them, however tired I may be. Even these days, when we are going from village to village trying to arouse a patriotic feeling among the people to prepare them for independence with meetings and speeches which sometimes last till very late at night, I always check myself and, when I am finally by myself, I faithfully give to prayer the appointed time before going to sleep. But last night, you remember, we had several mishaps. Our car had a puncture, it took time to get a spare wheel, we then missed our way and had to go back a good stretch, we lost much time and arrived very late at the village where we were supposed to have a public meeting. We wanted to go straight to bed, but the poor people were still there waiting for us through all that time, and I did not want to disappoint them. So we had our meeting, which took two or three hours, and I went to bed at an unusually late hour. So late it was that I didn't even think of my prayers at all, lay down and fell asleep at once. I must have been sleeping a couple of hours when I suddenly woke up with a start. The thought that I had omitted my prayers had come up through my sleep in my mind and had jerked me into a painful awakening. I felt desolate. If God is so good that he looks after me day by day with such unfailing providence, how can I be so mean that I can go through the day and finish it without thinking of him, without even saying my night prayers? Since then I have not slept, I have just been sitting miserably on my bed, and I feel all sorry and guilty."

Kalelkar—who, together with a deep religious faith and a total devotion to Gandhi had also a great sense of humor and an inexhaustible stock of moralizing stories—told him with respectful interest, "Far from me, Bapu, to enter your conscience, but will you allow me to tell you a story?" Gandhi, who his close associates called "Bapu," that is "father," answered with a sad smile: "You may go ahead." Kalelkar adopted his storyteller stand and began: "There was once a Sufi saint who would faithfully say his night prayers every day before retiring, but one day he forgot, and, when he was fast asleep, he noticed that someone was shaking him violently by the shoulder and was telling him, 'Come on, get up at once and say now your night prayers which you had forgotten.' He got up immediately and was going to start his prayers when he looked for a moment to see who it was that had woke him up, and to thank him. Imagine his surprise when, on looking carefully, he realized that the person that had woke him up was none other than Iblis, the devil, in person. He wanted to make sure, and asked him, 'Are you the devil?'—'Yes.'—'Then I don't understand this. I understood that the devil's role was to get people not to pray, and now I find that the devil himself wakes me up to remind me to say the prayers I had forgotten. I don't understand it.'—'I can explain everything. Yes, you are quite right in saying that my job is to get people to drop their prayers. In fact I did that with you only a few days ago. Do you remember? I made you sleepy and you went to bed without praying. Didn't it happen like that? Yes, and I felt very happy and proud of myself about it. But then something happened, and you will undoubtedly remember that too. The next morning, when you woke up and remembered that you had omitted your prayers the previous night, you felt such sorrow and contrition and did so much penance for it that you gained much more merit before God with your repentance than you would have gained with your prayers, and that does not go well with me, do you see that? So I don't want the same show today. Don't you wake up tomorrow with the remorse for not having prayed tonight and get again double merit, which makes me furious. Come on, be a good sport now, get up and pray as you have to, and no nonsense tomorrow about repentance and penance. Is it clear now?' With that,

Iblis left and the Sufi prayed. Everybody was satisfied. The Sufi learned his lesson about the value of penance in the spiritual life. The one who does not seem to have learned his lesson is Iblis himself, and he has made now the same mistake with you. He made you miss your prayers, but you have spent the night in vigil and atonement. His tactics have misfired again, and I guess he must be regretting by now he tackled the wrong person this time with his wiles. Don't you think so?" The Mahatma smiled his first smile that morning, and the campaign for independence went on village by village. The lesson of the parable is clear and useful. When Iblis gets a wrong result, he changes his approach. Good to know. It is enough to do the opposite of what he suggests, to go to the other end of the diameter, in order to counteract his attacks. Subtle rules of spiritual warfare.

If the presence of Iblis sounds too Mephistophelian, there is always the subconscious to appeal to. In practice it comes to the same thing. For all we know it may even have horns and hoofs the way the experts speak about it and common people imagine it. Essentially it is a matter of terminology, although the modern term sounds today more respectable. Let us take a very simple example. I have determined that I'll spend an hour in prayer each day. I even have the time marked in my timetable: 6 to 7. (In the evening, of course!) I begin. I get nowhere. Five minutes pass when I thought it was half an hour. I shake my watch. It's working all right. Only my mind is not working today. Just dull and distracted and dead. And my whole body is aching. Impossible to stand this for one minute more. And useless, anyhow. What am I getting by squatting here in an awkward semi-lotus half posture like a hungry fakir in search of alms? God certainly doesn't enjoy my posture. And neither do I. I could more profitably spend this time reading or working or just walking or resting. I am a busy man, and my time counts. And this is sheer hypocrisy anyway. I'm not praying, and I'm in a praying posture. Let me end the ordeal. Up I go. But wait a minute. There are directives on this point. Yes, right on it. And I unhappily remember them at the wrong time. The injunction is clear: When you feel like praying less, pray more. I feel like shortening the hour I had fixed, so now I am to go beyond the hour. Very well, then. Here I stay. And since I am to stay for a long time, better get reconciled to it and make a good job of a bad one. After all, this is not such an overwhelming calamity. I can stand that much. I won't move from here. And since I am here in a praying posture, I could even pray. Now that my mind knows it is stuck here for an hour, it may even resign itself and keep quiet and allow me to pray. Not so very hard. I've prayed much in my life, and I know how to do it. It's simple. I'm at it now. Time will now go much faster. Soon the hour and the overtime will be over. And if all goes well I may even skip the overtime!

The mind has the quality of the child. When it senses weakness, it attacks and insists and cries and kicks with overpowering fury. But when, in its infallible perception of persons and moods, it sees a firm stand and an immovable decision, it soon climbs down, reduces volume, calls back the agitation, and keeps quiet. It knows perfectly well that this is in its own best interest.

More than the tactics here involved, what is important is the attitude underlying them. The bending over backwards. The other end of the diameter. The turn. The twist. The awareness of a tendency in the mind that may vitiate a choice, and the promptness to correct it by asking God to take us precisely in the opposite direction. Another text from the Exercises in the introductory "Annotations": "If by any chance someone is unduly attached to something, he'll do well to change with all his possible strength, and come to desire the opposite. He must persist in prayer and all kind of spiritual exercises, and in asking God for the opposite of what he is attached to; protesting that he gives up his original intention and does not want it unless God removes his attachment and puts order in his desires." By asking God to do that, we put ourselves in the mood, the frame of mind, the anticipation that the choice we disliked (poverty in the standard example) is the one we are going to be required to make. That clears the air, prepares the process, unbends the mind—and the right decision can now be taken in freedom.

There is some similarity between this process and the way the method of "catastrophic expectation" works in therapy. A young man, for instance, fears he is going to fail in an examination, and that fear prevents him from sleeping, resting, thinking, living, and, of course, from studying and preparing properly for the examination. A counselor may then tell him something like this: Imagine that the worst has happened. You have failed in the exam. Fine. Everybody learns about it. So what? You lose one year. What is one year in a whole life? Go on mentioning and imagining and living vividly in your mind all the actual situations into which your failure is going to put you. Face them. Drink them in. Let them sink. Let them stink. And at the end of it all you're still alive, aren't you? Alive and kicking. And laughing at it all. What is there in a failure after all? Thousands have failed and have lived happily ever after. So can I. I can live with failure. I can recover my lost sleep and my appetite and my zest for living and I can even go back to my books and prepare for the examination. Who knows, I may pass it after all.

So long as the mind blindly opposes a situation, it blocks every system in the soul and prevents a solution. When, however, the mind is made to face and entertain and accept the feared calamity, the "catastrophic expectation," it ultimately resigns itself, relaxes, unbends, and clears the way for a sensible decision. That is also, under grace and with the singular blessing that accompanies the generosity of the soul toward God, the effect on the mind of the prayer "that our Lord may call us to actual poverty"—or to any unpleasant choice we fear. The prejudice has been removed. The repugnance has been overcome. The fear has been conquered. And that is essential news when we are speaking of choices. Because fear is the worst of advisers.

The Climate
of Elections

If fear is the worst enemy of a right choice, its best friend is peace. Peace of soul, tranquility, transparency. Clear sky and placid waters. When the stars can be seen and their positions can be checked and the route can be charted on the seas. Peace of mind in the midst of a troubled world. Hurry and agitation and pressure and anxiety are not the right atmosphere for a reliable choice.

Ignatius distinguishes two moods in the soul which he identifies in standard terminology: consolation and desolation. Consolation is "an inner movement . . . a burning love of God . . . tenderness unto tears . . . the inability to love anything in itself apart from God . . . the growing impulse of faith, hope, love and inner joy which bring peace and quiet to the soul." Words fail, but the experience is unmistakable. Indeed, Ignatius would be surprised and frustrated if a person who is going through his spiritual exercises would not experience such deep moods, high and low, and so he instructs the spiritual director to inquire and find out what is wrong. "When the person who is going through the exercises feels no internal movements in his soul, no consolation or desolation, the director must question him very closely to find out whether he follows the instructions, keeps the timetable and observes all the directives he has been given, asking for a detailed account in each of these things." The implication seems to be that if a person doesn't experience that deep play of spiritual moods over a protracted period of time in his or her prayer life, that person isn't really trying. Expert warning.

Desolation is "all the opposite . . . darkness in the soul, confusion, upsetting, tendency to anything low and base . . . uneasiness, anxiety and agitation . . . no faith, no hope, no love . . . only laziness and tepidity and sadness . . . as though the soul were separated from her Creator and Lord." A gloomy picture, which anybody engaged in the quest of the spirit knows to be only too real.

The interesting point is that immediately after the description, Ignatius records the warning that concerns us here: "In time of desolation don't make any change." Obvious advice, and yet often forgotten. Ignatius hastens to give it, because he knows that to be the most practical and important conclusion of the study of moods in the soul: the way they affect our choices. And he knows too how often we ignore what ordinary common sense tells us. Negative feelings are not good counselors at the time of making a decision. Darkness is not the time to change one's way through the forest. Go on or rest where you are, but don't change your course in the fog. Wait for the morning, the sunshine, a clear sky and an unimpeded visibility. Then you'll change if you must. Not now. Not under the cloud. Not in "desolation."

And yet that is what most people do. At least most of my students. When they join college after school they are faced with a teasing choice: whether to take as medium of instruction for their university degree their mother tongue, Gujarati, or the world language, English. The choice is theirs—

and the bewilderment also theirs. Clear advantages and nagging disadvantages both ways. Hard to change suddenly from the Gujarati medium in school to the English medium at college. Loss of cultural contact with tradition, and fear that marks in the first examinations will be lower and the final result impaired. On the other hand, the lure of English, the window to the world, and its job advantages. And the social pressures one way and the other. From home and society and their own friends. No easy decision. They know they have to make it, but there is plenty of time to decide; then the time approaches, our college offers both media, and all the freshman has to do is to check off the proper square in the proper entry on the admission form: medium. He hesitates. He delays. He goes back home. He consults. He prays. He asks his friends. He asks everybody. He asks his former teachers. He asks his future teachers. Some say one thing, some say another. I tell him the mother tongue is best. Others tell him the opposite. Finally the last date to submit the form comes, and he marks one choice: English. He'll manage it. Others with less brains and worse preparation have done it, so why can't he? He comes bold and confident to the first lecture delivered entirely in English. And he panics. He doesn't follow a word. He can't tell at the end whether the professor was talking physics or mathematics or maybe it was economics after all. And if the first day he hasn't understood a word, the second day he won't either. He'll be lost. He'll get nowhere. He'll lose the year and maybe the degree. He doesn't sleep that night. Next day he comes early to the college office with an application to change his medium. He tells the principal that he has realized the cultural advantages of the mother tongue in education. He pays the additional fee for the late change. He goes back to the familiar medium. And he suffers because he does not appreciate the educational advantages of the mother tongue, and secretly envies those of his companions who have made the change and

79

have stuck to it. I'm not concerned here with the conflicting claims of languages, but with the mechanics of a choice badly made. If only the freshman had had the courage to stand his ground at the first onslaught of panic, he would have made good his original choice. And would have saved his fee.

I know because I went through the experience myself. When I arrived in India I hardly knew any English. I landed in the mathematics honors course of Madras University which had a Brahminical tradition of mathematical excellence and lived up to it in the talent of its students, the brilliance of its professors and the speed of their lectures. I sat through the first one, and when the professor left after an hour of scholarly disquisitions, I was as wise in calculus as when he had entered. I had only copied furiously in my notebook every single word he had written on the blackboard, not those he had spoken which I couldn't even approximate, but just what he wrote on the board. But then I didn't let anybody know I hadn't followed. I smiled broadly and told kind inquirers that the first day had been swell, thanks, and the lectures were magnificent and I was sure I would have a good time and a useful year. I did. And a lively one too. Not an idle moment. The joyful discoveries of words first and sentences later, the surprise of finding myself hearing and understanding, the growing confidence, the final familiarity. I played my role so well that once, in the midst of my days of ignorance, when a professor himself did not know the pronunciation of an English word, he deferentially asked me in the middle of the class and before everybody to be so kind as to supply him with the right pronunciation. I had the only pale skin in the midst of that most beautiful of exact tans that is the privilege of South Indian Brahmins, and he took my white skin as an evident sign of my being British—at a time when Spain was not even in the Common Market! I was taken by surprise, but recovered in time to hold my bluff; I stood up respectfully and uttered, with the British aplomb I was supposed to possess, whatever sounds came first to my lips. They all nodded wisely, and my pronunciation became official. The language battle was won. One day I would even write books in English.

The patient courage to hold on to a decision reasonably made is an essential part of the art of choosing. It is not stubbornness, blindness, obdurateness, but the wisdom to wait out the night and keep on and trust the first choice—which is trusting oneself. Without that trust there is no firm choice and no steady life.

Tagore says that we all need a camel in our lives. A horse is fine for beauty and strength and speed and breed, to enjoy a ride and run a race and win a prize. All very very fine. But then there are deserts also in life, and there the best of horses is of no use, and speed of no avail. The horse will grow impatient and restless and its hoofs will sink in the sand and its breath will burn in the heat, and it will run wild and fall and die in the ruthless sand. Horses are not for deserts. But camels are. The camel will set on its route and will keep on and on and on. Even without food, without water, without reins, without direction, it will go on steadily, faithfully, reliably, and will keep its course and cross the desert and reach the waters and save itself and its rider. The dogged perseverance to keep to one's course steadily in the worst circumstances is a prized asset for survival in this world. We all need a camel in our stables.

The right climate for an election is peace and joy. The cloudless sky. The unimpeded vision. The balanced mind. The contented soul. The good angel. The Holy Spirit. The spirit of peace and joy and consolation and the wisdom to sense the will of God in our lives and accept it and do it. With the light and the strength of the Spirit the doubtful choice becomes evident, and the impossible decision an easy step.

The Art of Choosing

"The kingdom of heaven is like treasure lying buried in a
field. The man who found it, buried it again; and for sheer
joy went and sold everything he had, and bought that field"
(Matt. 13:44). The key word is "joy." For the joy of it. For
sheer joy. No calculating, no hesitating. No waiting and no
planning. Joy takes over and the impossible is done in a
flash. People will think me mad. They always do on such
occasions. And I respect them, but I go my contented way
because I've seen what they haven't seen, what I myself had
not seen before, what I could not have seen if someone in his
mercy had not shown it lovingly to me. There is gold in that
field. I've seen it now with my own eyes. There is joy in
poverty and there is bliss in sacrifice and there is fulfillment
in working for the poor. I know it, and so my choice is obvious and my satisfaction complete.

Spiritual joy facilitates our choices because of the detach-
ing quality it has and brings to bear on our addicted hearts. I
know my attachments. And I know I have others I don't
know. I've tried to neutralize those I know by the tactics I've
learned, by prayer and examination and self-control and
bending over to the other side. Yet I sense them still there
staining my glasses and tilting my scales. The attachment
remains attached. I don't know what to do further. And then
comes joy. Sudden and unexpected and overwhelming and
sweeping over everything. And the attachments just drain
away in the flood. Who cares about bodily pleasures or
earthly possessions when the tide of another joy fills up every recess in the mind and lifts the heart and inaugurates
heaven in the soul! The right perspective is essential to the
right choice, and joy has the power to change the perspective
with ease. Joy is the climate of heaven.

Makarand Dave, mystic and friend, has said deeply and
experientially: "We don't achieve detachment; it happens to
us." I may pull for all I'm worth to make my mind come
unstuck from an unholy attachment it fancies. Brute force

82

achieves nothing. A thousand efforts and no result. But then comes the gentle touch of joy. A hint, a whisper, a whiff of a distant perfume in the breeze. And the soul perceives it and shudders for joy and pulls itself free and takes flight and soars and finds its true direction in the sky. If money was the test example of attachment, Matthew and Zacchaeus, who knew the value of money and watched their gains, testify with their ready turn of life to the overwhelming power of a presence, a call, and the bursting of joy into their lives. Money just ceased to be a value for them. A lifelong attachment evaporated in a moment of joy. People who knew them wondered at their apparently thoughtless actions. But they had been visited by joy and they knew they were right in their surprise moves. They must have been the talk of the town for quite some time.

Ignatius wrote to Borgia, duke, viceroy, and saint: "The most direct way of finding God [for Ignatius "finding God" and "finding the will of God" were synonyms] is that in which God our Lord communicates himself more by his very holy gifts and his spiritual graces [which again is Ignatian terminology for consolation and spiritual joy]. On our part it is a great help to us, aided by his divine grace, to search and experiment in numerous ways, in order to find and walk in the way which is the clearest, the happiest, the most blissful here on earth, wholly directed and ordained to eternal life, and in this way we find ourselves surrounded and penetrated by these very holy gifts. By these gifts I mean those that it is not in our power to have at our pleasure, but which are granted solely by the mighty giver of all good gifts. Such gifts are, when we place ourselves in the perspective of God's Majesty, faith, hope, very intense charity, joy and spiritual repose, tears, intense consolation, elevation of spirit, divine impressions and illuminations, and all other spiritual tastes and sentiments relative to such gifts. We are convinced in our deepest selves that without them our thoughts, words, and works are impure, cold and restless; thus, in order that they may become warm, clear and active for the greater service of God, we ought to desire these gifts, wholly or in part, and these spiritual graces, insofar as they can help us for the greater glory of God.

Francis Xavier wrote to Goa from Mylapore in Madras how he himself had gone about making an important decision: "In this holy house of St. Thomas I made it my business to pray to God that he would let me feel in my soul his most holy will, being determined myself to carry it out, as he who gives the inclination will also give the strength to follow it. God, in his wonted mercy, did remember me, and it was with great interior consolation that I felt and knew his will to be that I should go to Macassar. I am sure that God our Lord is going to show me much mercy in this journey, as he has made me feel with such great satisfaction of my soul and spiritual consolation that this is his most holy will. I am fully determined to carry out what God has made me feel in my soul, and, were I not to do it, I would feel I was going against his will." He knew the terminology and he knew the method. Spiritual consolation. Interior joy. Feeling God's will in his soul. And the strength to carry it out. Xavier took his decisions in the joy of the Spirit. He had learned well.

Ignatius comes down to the practical ways of making an important choice, and he proposes three. The first is "when God our Lord so moves and attracts the soul that without even a chance to doubt, the said devout soul follows the way shown to her, as St. Paul and St. Matthew did." This may seem remote to us, but was not so for Ignatius. In fact, when setting down later in the official "Constitutions" of the Society of Jesus, which he had founded, the ways in which the general of the Jesuits is to be elected, he begins by legislating as follows: "If all those who are to elect the new general feel a common inspiration to choose someone before any ballots are cast, let him be general. The Holy Spirit, who has moved them to such an election, will easily make up for all the procedures and formalities required." He was open to that direct action of the Holy Spirit on the soul, and was consistent with himself in setting down as legislation what he believed in faith to be possible. No general, however, has been elected that way.

The second way proposed by Ignatius to make a choice: "When sufficient clarity is gained through the experience of consolations and desolations." Here the repeated play of light and darkness in the soul, observed with insight and sensitivity, points the way toward the right choice. A friend of mine had his own interpretation of this method. The question for him was whether to smoke or not to smoke, and the help he found in this procedure was, according to him, definite. He said to me: "Wonderful how this system works. It's all so clear to me now. When I smoke, I get consolation, and when I stop smoking I get desolation. Clear, isn't it? I must go on smoking." I pointed out to him that in my opinion that was not exactly what St. Ignatius had in mind when he devised that method. There was a question with him of a subtler play at a deeper level. Something Ignatius himself had felt when convalescent in the Loyola homestead. He had noticed that when imagining in his idle hours the military exploits he would perform and the love adventures he would carry out, he enjoyed the fantasy so long as he was in it, but was left empty and dejected after it; whereas, on the contrary, when he imagined the great things he was going to do for Christ, as St. Francis and St. Dominic had done, he was left glowing and contented even after the thought had passed. That is where he learned his own method and began to be sensitive to the ways of the Spirit. Ignatius made much of sensitivity. In practice this means thinking of a choice before the Lord in prayer, holding up the several options before his loving eye, and paying attention to our own true feelings while we do that. When do we feel happy, at ease, contented; and when troubled, uneasy, dissatisfied? This exercise, lovingly repeated, may lead to the focussing of joy, genuine spiritual joy, on the true choice.

Ignatius' third way: This includes a number of rules and procedures, but the central point is just the study and contrast of reasons for and against. The usual way in which we proceed. The detailed study. The special commission. The report. The discussion. The careful listing and weighing and comparing and judging. The reasons in favor are stronger: Do it. The reasons against are weightier: Don't do it. All agree. The decision is clear. Sealed and proclaimed. If anybody asks why this decision was taken, we have the answer ready and the list of reasons drawn up. That is how we proceed in practice; that is what we call the rational and sensible way to act. Our way of making decisions is universally this third one.

The curious fact is that such was not the case with Ignatius. It is historically, exegetically, and characteristically true that with Ignatius this third way was only an exception to be used only if and when the first two happened to fail, which should not normally be the case. He did list reasons for and against when he had to decide on something, but that was a sort of preliminary homework with him, not the actual choice. For the actual choice he expected God "to move my will," "to place (note the verb) the right choice in my soul," so that "the impulse that rules my choice should come from above," and I may feel that "the attraction or rejection comes only from God." All these verbal quotations are, curiously and almost contradictorily enough, from the third method, from the rational listing of advantages and disadvantages, and thus they give an idea of the degree to which a choice for Ignatius went far beyond reason and study into faith and prayer and devotion and love. "The impulse to choose must come from above . . . from the love of God." Every choice is love.

A deeper way of comparing the three methods is to realize that essentially the three are one, and it is God who speaks in the three of them: in the first in a direct unmistakable way as God and Lord of the human heart; in the second through the spiritual moods of the soul which he rules and directs to focus the eye of the mind on the beneficial choice; and in the third through his silence which is also message and communication (the thought is Karl Rahner's), signaling to the soul to go ahead on its own lights, with the faith and certainty that God, who alone can tell the soul how to proceed, will direct the election of which he has chosen the method.

And then, the "confirmation." It is not enough to make a decision; it has to be "confirmed." And this is no mere formality, no spiritual red tape, no supernatural rubber stamp. The whole decision is in abeyance pending its confirmation. "Once the election and deliberation is over, the person who has gone through it must resort to prayer with full earnestness before God our Lord, and offer to him his election so that his Divine Majesty may receive it and confirm it, if that be his greater service and glory."

A page from Ignatius' diary will explain what that confirmation is and how much it places us again in the close intimacy with God which the process of election entails. The entry is dated 18-12-1544. "Later while preparing the altar and vesting I had a strong impulse to say: 'Eternal Father, confirm me; Eternal Son, confirm me; Eternal Spirit, confirm me; Holy Trinity, confirm me; my only God, confirm me!' I said this with great earnestness and with much devotion and tears, very often repeated and very interiorly felt. Saying 'Eternal Father, will you not confirm me? . . .' I said Mass without tears. Had some thoughts without any shedding or abundance of tears, which pained me and robbed me of devotion, and moved me in some way or other not to be satisfied with the lack of confirmation in the last Mass of the

Trinity. I became impatient [the original says 'furious'] with the Trinity. [Continues the next day:] I finished the Mass and spent a short time in vocal prayer: 'Eternal Father, confirm me . . . ,' with a flood of tears spreading over my face. Today, even as I walked through the city, with much joy of soul, I represented the Most Holy Trinity to myself. I felt confirmed about the past."

On reading those words I come to realize with unavoidable clarity and full appreciation how far remote that spiritual discernment and almost mystical experience is from the purely clever decisions and sophisticated choices that prevail today in the managerial world, and even in religious management. There is a whole world of decision-making, computer simulation, games theory, linear programming. I've taught some of those subjects in my mathematics class, and personally enjoy them immensely. They are useful procedures, and modern management is based on them. They are important tools of corporate progress. But they are only that: tools. We in religious life do well to take advantage of all that is best, of all that can help to enhance our resources and foster our work. And we are fairly prompt in adopting modern means and harnessing technology to our services. The danger is that technology may replace spirituality, and a brainstorming session may be taken for discernment in the Spirit. Efficiency is to be sought—so long as it doesn't replace charism.

The climax of God's action in the soul is, in Ignatian terminology, the "consolation without a cause." When God "comes in and out and moves the soul and sets it fully in the love of his Divine Majesty." With a preceding cause, he says, anybody can bring joy to the soul; but without it, it is only God, Lord and Master, who can thus recreate the souls he has made. And in that exclusive of God's touches, Ignatius makes bold to assert, "there is no possible error, as it comes solely from God." This is a bold stand, a courageous claim, an act of faith in "the God whose consolation never fails us" of Paul in 2 Cor. 1:3. God is the Lord of joy, and in the sudden, unmixed, undeserved tide of joy that enters the soul unbidden and unexpected we recognize his retinue, his glory, his presence. Joy brings its own certainty and doesn't need credentials from anybody else; it is God's visiting card. God rides in the wind of the "consolation without a cause." And he who has experienced it, knows it.

And immediately, a warning. Timely and essential in handling the supreme experience of joy in the Spirit. "When the consolation is without cause, there is no mistake possible as has been said; yet, the person that has been favored with it will do well to watch and check very carefully the actual time of the consolation and distinguish it from the subsequent glow in which the soul thinks and decides by itself, reaching conclusions which may not come from God." The danger of overenthusiasm, of mixed cues, of attributing to God what is merely a discourse of the mind. The repeated complaint among genuine men of the spirit: I was absolutely sure that was God's will for me . . . and yet how has it so obviously misfired? How have I been so obviously misled? Can't I trust my discernments any more? You certainly can, with the risk and the thrill and the challenge a choice always entails, provided you sharpen your sight and watch the frontiers and draw the boundaries. And never mind mistakes. Readiness to see them is the best school of discernment.

A case in the gospel: If anyone around Jesus was likely to be carried away by his enthusiasm, that was Peter. He did so more than once. And then he learned moderation and restraint. At Caesarea Philippi, Peter received a direct revelation from the Father beyond all flesh and blood, that made him burst into the purest profession of faith in Christ's person and divinity: "You are the Messiah, the Son of the living God!" And Jesus himself showed his appreciation and rewarded his commitment with an appointment and a promise: "You are Peter, the Rock, and on this rock I will build my church." That was the high point of Peter's "consolation," and he enjoyed it to the full. But soon he unwittingly abused it. When, the next moment, Jesus began to unburden himself before the newly proclaimed faith of his first disciple, and to speak of the passion and death that awaited him shortly, Peter, still in the afterglow of the revelation of the Father, took it upon himself to dissuade Jesus from such absurd thoughts of suffering and death; and, taking him by the arm with an unthinkable touch of excessive familiarity began to "rebuke him": "Heaven forbid! No, Lord, this shall never happen to you." And now Jesus had something quite different to tell him from the preceding promise and commendation: "Away with you, Satan! You are a stumbling block to me. You think as men think, not as God thinks." Note the contrast. Peter who had just spoken "what no mere man" could have told him, speaks now precisely "as mere men" speak. And he doesn't realize it. He has overstepped the boundary. He has passed from the moment when the Father was speaking in him to the moment when his own human considerations were speaking in him. And he doesn't notice it. But Jesus does and takes him up sharply. He calls him "Satan." Peter must have taken some time to figure out exactly what had happened. In fact at Mount Tabor he took a similar attitude. The light of Jesus' face, the shining of his vestments and the presence of Moses and Elijah carried him to his wonted enthusiasm, and then his own inclination took over and made him say: "Let us make tents and stay here." The wrong suggestion. He had not yet learned his lesson. Then in a moment of intimacy with the risen Christ he no doubt felt intensely the love and devotion to his leader and master that were his very life; yet, when asked about his love he grew prudent and answered: "Lord, you know everything; you know that I love you." He knew now how to keep his limits and say the right thing.

One example of my experience. A zealous priest felt, at a time of prayer and recollection, a great love for the people he worked for, and he couldn't but feel strongly that it was God himself who inspired in him such a selfless and apostolic love. In the wake of that experience he took a resolution to devote three hours each evening to visit from house to house the people he worked for and genuinely loved. He began to do so with great zeal. Soon, however, he got tired. He scolded himself for being remiss in doing what he had seen so clearly to be the will of God. He kept at it with dogged perseverance. Then little by little he began to realize that he was hating the very people he went to visit under the obligation he had laid on himself to visit them. A project that had started in love was ending in hate. What had gone wrong? The boundary. Clear to any experienced eye, but blurred still for him. The impulse to love his people was directly from God; the decision to visit them three hours daily was from his own mind. Only the proximity of the two movements legitimized the second and conferred on it a seal of authenticity it did not merit. If he had realized it was his own decision, he could have reasonably altered it as experience guided. But he had thought the inspiration came directly from God, and so he felt guilty and fearful and frustrated when he couldn't keep it up. A timely distinction would have saved him much self-recrimination.

Young men who have made the Spiritual Exercises as a preparation to choosing a way of life may be surprised to know that Ignatius deliberately forbids the director to incline or influence or predispose the retreatant in any way in favor of religious life. When I made such a retreat at the end of my school days, the director read out to us in full with apparent honesty the stern admonition of Ignatius restraining him as director from any such action. He added: You see, then, that you need not be afraid of me; my hands are tied and my lips are sealed in this matter. But that was only a clever ruse to make us lower our defenses and render us docile when the attack would come. In fact he spent almost entirely the five days he had at his disposal proving with effective eloquence that the only sensible thing for us to do was to go and join the novitiate. Twelve out of a group of forty did. A wicked thought occurs to me as I write this: How many of those twelve remain? I don't know it myself, and anyhow I wouldn't blame an overzealous retreat master for the personal failures of his charges. I'm only warning again, with Ignatius, of the danger of overenthusiasm when it comes to making decisions in life.

The reason for this prohibition to interfere, however, goes far beyond overenthusiasm into a much deeper and richer realm. And that will take another chapter.

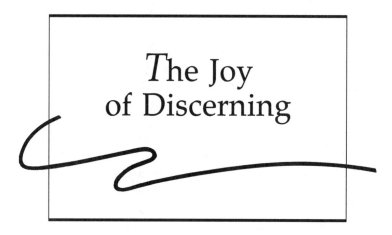

The Joy
of Discerning

This is the text of the prohibition to interfere, in its most relevant section: "It is much more convenient, indeed far better in every way in this search of the divine will, that the Lord and Creator should deal himself with the soul committed to him, embracing it in love and glory, and leading it along the way it can best serve him. The director is not to show preference for one choice or the other, but to remain in the middle like the needle in the scales. Let him allow the Creator to deal directly with his creature, and the creature with its Creator and Lord."

These are beautiful words. And daring ones. No wonder Ignatius had trouble with the Inquisition about them. God is expected to deal directly ("without third parties" is the actual word in the text) with the person, and the person with God. He is Creator and Lord, and can do it and does it. And that is, in the last analysis, the essence of the human choice in love and under faith: God acting in the soul and leading it gently, lovingly, powerfully, and freely toward the separate choices that make up and prepare the fundamental choice of man for his supreme good. And the soul open, ready, attuned to God's action, nodding at every indication and bending at every command, supple and willing before the leanings of the Spirit. The Creator and his creature. God and the soul. He and I. Exalted privilege and humble reality. Nothing less is our patrimony in faith and submission, and in the boldness and confidence to make ours the blessings God is only too eager to bestow on us.

The art of choosing, like any other art, has to be learned through practice and reading and asking others and making mistakes and gathering experience . . . till it is mastered and becomes second nature, spontaneous, instinctive, connatural, like driving a car or playing the violin or programming a computer. Rules have to be learned in order to go beyond the rules, and procedures have to be mastered in order to be able to ignore them. Any good professional acquires that skill and depends on it for success in his or her profession. We should not do less in ours.

If I am alive today, and I certainly am, I owe it to the professional skill and clinical sense of a great doctor and a great man. His name was Dr. Cook, and he had come from his native New Zealand as a Salvation Army missionary to practice surgery and to witness to Christ in the Emery Hospital at Anand where I was studying Gujarati at the time. His power to diagnose was as celebrated throughout the region as his apostolic zeal and direct simplicity in speaking to one and all of the love of Jesus he had in his heart. He was as skillful at handling the scalpel in the operation theater as at playing the trumpet at evangelical meetings, and his powerful and loving personality dominated the social life of the small country town for years. Just as well for me. It was to his hospital that I was taken when suddenly one evening I experienced a sharp piercing pain in the lower abdomen. Dr. Cook had gone out, as he did every evening, to hold a prayer meeting in a neighboring village, and would not return till late at night. He would see me next morning, they told me.

Meanwhile another doctor examined me, diagnosed hepatic colic, wrote it in the report, gave me sedatives, and laid me to sleep in a makeshift bed they set up in Dr. Cook's own office, as there was not a single bed free (there never was) in the hospital. I remained alone, and, in my desire not to burden others, declined the company of the infirmarian who had volunteered to stay with me for the night. They all left and closed the door behind them. After a while—I do not know how long—the pain shot through my whole body with a throbbing intensity that tied my muscles and numbed my senses. I needed help. I cried faintly. Nobody came. I lowered myself onto the floor. I tried to crawl. I collapsed on the floor. A nurse on her rounds then entered the room, saw me, gave me a penicillin shot, and summoned Dr. Cook at dead of night. I saw him come as an angel of hope out of a cloud of suffering. He was given the report the other doctor had written on me, glanced at it and threw it aside. He felt my body. Then he leaned gently on my face and said, "Give me your breath." I exhaled. He sniffed. Immediately he stood up and issued orders like a general on campaign: "Typical smell. Acute appendicitis. No time to lose. No tests. Operation theater one. Total anesthetics." Days later, when I had lost my appendix and regained my strength, he commented on the operation and told me, "Thank the Lord for your life, Father. Your appendix had burst. A little longer and you were a dead man. We moved just in time." And he added rather disconcertingly, "By the way, I must thank you for the good time you gave me with the operation. I had never seen such a big appendix and with so many complications in my life: swollen, infected, and perforated. It was such a pleasure to operate! You gave me a real treat!" I managed to say that I was always happy to give satisfaction; and happier of course to be alive. And I owed it to his infallible sense of diagnosis. Beyond any textbook and ahead of any symptoms, without any time and against the written report of the other doctor, with a mere sniff and a clinical eye, he had sensed the ailment and named the cause. The scalpel did the rest. And I lived to tell the story and celebrate the infallible skill of an extraordinary doctor and a wonderful man.

A diagnosis is a choice. Identify the agent. Pick out the real cause. Define the actual illness among a thousand possible ones. Study, ask, investigate, compare. By all means prepare yourself as best you can. And then follow the hunch that years of practice and a wealth of experience have led you to formulate in the recess of your mind. A mere sniff of the breath against a hundred textbooks. That kind of hunch, educated and cultivated through study and reflection, and liberated through spontaneity and freedom, can be a most valuable guide to a right choice. It can save a person's life.

As a lifelong teacher of mathematics I know the value of hunches in my profession. We live on them. Again here there is the indispensable process and drill and information and mastery of methods and results and research. There are books and studies on every conceivable branch of mathematics, books on problems, on solutions of problems, and on how to go about finding solutions of problems. All that is needed. But then the moment comes to face an original problem and tackle it and find its solution. There all the training becomes background, and out of it emerges the stray thought, the isolated hint, the wild hunch that no textbook contains and no teacher explains, and it opens a new trail, clears all obstacles and produces the solution, neat and exact and evident. An imaginative approach can be faster and more effective than all the classroom routine which consists only of solving again problems which have already been solved.

I have read of an antiquary who could date an old table, painting, statuette more accurately through the instinct he had developed through years of practice than all his colleagues could do with carbon tests and exhaustive catalogues and chemical treatment and the latest research. A serious professional does develop in the exercise of his profession a special sense, an inner instinct, an expert touch, that enable him to make decisions and reach conclusions in the field of his speciality with far greater speed and accuracy and reliability than anybody outside his field. That is why it is his profession. Our field is the Spirit, and to know, identify, discern, follow his leads should become second nature with us.

St. Paul claimed confidently: "We are those who have the mind of Christ" (1 Cor. 2:16). Beautiful result of the love and faith and prayer and friendship that unite us with Jesus in daily contact through years and through life, molding our tastes, directing our choices, shaping our mind more and more into the very mind of Christ. Familiarity with Holy Scripture in prayer and study is the best background to Christian choices. To know instinctively what will please our friend is the best fruit of friendship. We don't need now in every case to go through the procedures, to follow all the steps, to draw up the lists and weigh the reasons and observe and discern. Or we may still do all that, but with a light heart and an easy mind, because all the time we have the answer within us. We know. As the wife knows the moods of her husband even before he speaks. By affinity, by connaturality, by living together and being one family. We are one family, the family of the Father with Christ in the Spirit, and as such we know the family ways. That is discernment.

Jesus said it most beautifully: "The sheep follow their shepherd because they know his voice" (John 10:4). The sheep may hear a thousand voices, but among them they will infallibly recognize the unique voice of their Good Shepherd and follow him. We have been listening to his voice through our lives. We know his voice as a child knows his mother's voice. Even before he knows the meaning of what his mother is saying, before he knows any grammar or any vocabulary, the child knows it is his mother who speaks and he senses the accent and guesses the mood and gets the message. The word of God has fallen in our ears much before we could understand it with our heads, we have been listening to the Holy Scriptures much before we knew their meaning; but their sound, their tune, their sense have molded our minds and guided our lives. And then little by little we have learned the vocabulary and mastered the grammar. God's language is our language, and his mind is our mind. We have also heard his word through his ministers, his representatives, his Church; through other Christians and dialogue and books; through the culture we inherit and the history we learn. And, above all, we have listened to his voice in our hearts, in prayer and silence and recollection and guidance, in the warnings of our conscience and the instincts of our behavior, in light and shadows, in encouragement and repentance. We know his voice. We know its ring, its tone, its loving echoes, and its unique modulation. We are his sheep. We know our shepherd's voice. And the voice of the shepherd marks the way for his sheep to go.

One of my Gujarati books has a daring subject: Shri Krishna's flute. Its title is a single word: *Murli,* the flute. And there is no need in India to specify whose flute it is. Every Hindu knows it, as he knows and senses and enjoys the depth and the beauty and the musicality of the theological symbol. The flute. The gentle sound. The light touch. The delicate blowing. And the notes dancing on the wings of the breeze. The forest of Vrindavan is large and deep, full of the thousand voices of birds and animals and the thunder in the storm and the rustling of the leaves in the wind. Symbol of the world with its cares and its worries and its demands on our attention and its drowning of the promptings of the heart in the noises of life. Many travelers cross the forest. Many walk through the jungle of noise. Some hear nothing in their hurry, some fear the roaring of the tiger and the hissing of the snake, some follow the voices of men to find the path to the nearest village. Some are lost. Some die on the way to nowhere. Some wander and wander around from sound to sound, from trail to trail. But for those who have ears to hear and love to want to hear, for the milkmaids of Mathura who think only of the beloved, and above all for Radha in her devotion and consecration and dedication to the master of her heart with the totality of her being, there is another sound that pierces through all other sounds and reaches the ear and touches the heart, clear and insistent and playful and demanding: The flute. Neat and unmistakable and true. A message, a direction, a call. And Radha stops whatever she is doing and starts in the direction of the sound, and flies and pines and longs and reaches in joy. The ability to recognize the sound of the flute among all other sounds: That is discernment. And its basis is love.

The Hindus have another beautiful symbol of discernment: The swan. The mythical swan had the characteristic that when drinking milk mixed with water it would drink only the milk and leave the water. That is why the art of discernment is called in Sanskrit "the science of the water and the milk," and why the white swan, pure and majestic and aloof in the clear waters, is its symbol and its model. The soul itself is called "the swan" (hans), and the highest type of religious ascetic is called "the supreme swan" (param-hans). That discernment by one's very nature, by spontaneous action, by the touch of the beak that signifies the sharp and clear edge of knowledge on the mixture of things that is this world, was such a fundamental value with the ancient Hindus that they chose that very name for the highest sannyasis. Such was Shri Ramakrishna Paramhans: "The Supreme Swan." The name of his disciple Swami Vivekananda is also known to the world, but what many in the world may not know is that the word "Vivek" in his name means precisely "discernment," which was the name a royal friend and devout maharaja gave him for his innate sense of spiritual discernment. "Vivekananda" means "Joy in Discernment." Beautiful name. I can lawfully turn it around: "discernment through joy." It is in the joy of the Spirit that true discernment takes place.

If the power of the swan is mythical, every migrating bird has the real and mysterious power of discerning the times and the tides, of locating stars and constellations, of guessing directions and landmarks and paths in the sky, and flying and flying for days and days, and landing in the exact ancestral spot at the predestined time each recurring year to the wonder and the joy of the people of the land who wait for their feathered friends to bring in the new spring in unfailing tryst. What genetic code of life-instinct wakes up inside the bird when the day comes, which only nature knows, and stirs its very vitals and makes it leave the comfort of its nest and take wing and hit the sky and set the course and gauge the distance and find a new home on the distant shore of a remote climate? No calculation, no planning, no clockwork can tell time and place. Only nature knows. And the bird, wholly and placidly in the arms of nature, knows it too. And migration takes place. Discernment with wings. Election in the sky. Choices by instinct. That is how nature works. And grace builds on nature. If only we know how to trust the Spirit and follow its urgings within us. Then the miracle of migration to promised lands will take place in our lives.

Now Ignatius' own comparison. In the same line of secret dealings between God and the soul. And in the same line of nature teaching spirit. The mystical touch. The family trait. The action of the Holy Spirit on the soul that thirsts for him, "like a drop of water entering a sponge": gentle, light, soft. The opposite of "a drop of water hitting a stone": harsh and loud and hurting. Familiarity between God and the soul is what makes for the easy contact, the obvious recognition, the instant understanding. The sponge is born in the water, as the soul is born in the Spirit, and as such it recognizes its presence, invites its coming, welcomes its touch. It need not ask for guarantees, examine credentials, or test identities. It knows. The soul recognizes the visit of the Spirit who enters it "in silence and peace, as coming to his own house through an open door." The promptings of the Spirit bring to the docile soul peace and silence and joy, and in that very peace and joy the soul detects their origin and readily follows them. The wrong proposition, however appealing it may sound at first, soon causes uneasiness and fear and trouble. Ignatius uses a word which is used in modern communication theory as a technical term to denote disturbances in the electronic world; he uses it in a way that is quite different, but still significant and symbolic of the spiritual communication of which he speaks. The word is "noise." The wrong proposal produces "noise" in the soul, like a poor transmission in a radio or a faulty circuit in a satellite. It blurs and disturbs and confuses and annoys. Any good electronics expert recognizes it for what it is and knows how to neutralize it. The true signal is clear and quiet and steady. A single dot on the radar screen. That is the Spirit.

I'm going to interpret in this light three hints which Ignatius gives for a good election; these hints, if viewed only superficially, may appear either theatrical or uncouth, but in a larger perspective—which I believe to be the true one—acquire a very relevant modernity and genuine significance. One hint is to think of the hour of my death, to see myself about to die, and imagine what, at that moment of truth, I would like to have chosen now. Which option, of the ones that confront me now, will make me feel happier at the moment of my death when I review my life at the last hour? Think of it, and take it, because that is the right option. This simplistic consideration can be abused, and *has* been freely abused from the pulpit to herd generous young people into ways of indiscriminate sanctity and a gregarious vocation to religious life as the choice that would obviously give greater joy to everybody at the hour of death. Even a mediocre preacher, given the right atmosphere and my own naive cooperation, can make me feel that at the hour of my death I certainly will like to have been a religious, a priest, a saint, an ascetic, an indefatigable worker, a fervent man of prayer, apostle and mystic, virgin and martyr all in one. My spiritual father at school, and this is another holy memory, directed us to meditate on death every Monday of the year, and used to repeat to us that the flickering light of the candle placed according to the traditional rite in the right hand of the dying man, was the clearest light on earth by which to see our path and make our choices through life. Well-meant rhetoric. But that is not the point. That is cheap, besides being morbid. In Sanskrit there is an expression for it: *'shmashan vairagya,'* which means "graveyard sanctity" or "tombstone asceticism" or "giving up the world at the cemetery," and which in the true wisdom, gentle irony, and fine linguistic sense of the Hindu sages exposes the weakness of the "graveyard method" of election. I realize that my spiritual father at school didn't know Sanskrit. Not his fault, of course. But there is a much deeper sense in the thought of death at the moment of making a choice, which is comfortably congruent with the spirituality of discernment I am describing here. Death is the moment when life is summed up, when the final perspective is gained; when all makes sense, painful and absurd though it may be, but radical and inevitable. I'm not speaking of the actual psychological experience of dying, which I haven't gone through yet, but of the meaning, the theology, the message and projection of the last act of man's existence on earth over the whole of it. In that supreme moment man's life stands before him as a whole, he sees himself as he has been, as he could have been, as he wanted to be, chances missed and opportunities made good use of, the totality of his experiences and the succession of his choices, the sum of his days and the fruit of his life. The painter has finished his portrait, has laid down his brush, steps back for a moment and takes a look at the finished work. And then he sees: That line, that shade, that color. It fits—or it doesn't. He may change it or not. Others will notice it or not. But he knows. He realizes in a flash that that stroke was out of place, that it doesn't go with the picture. That it doesn't fit. That is judgment. That is discernment. For the painter with the finished picture. For mortal man with his consummated existence. And for pilgrim man with his half-lived life and his half-drawn picture, to project in his mind for a moment the final image he wants and foresees, to stand back awhile, to look at the picture in his mind and at the choice at hand, and to take an option and set it on the picture and say with obvious evidence: it fits: or it doesn't. This choice I'm going to make goes well with my life, is part of my landscape, matches with the whole. Or it jars, it is out of place, it doesn't belong here. The artist can tell at a glance. Man in his sincerity can feel it in an instant. This goes well with me. Or it doesn't. The totality of my life, reflected at long range in the mirror of my death, is the perfect existential setting for the making of the right election.

The second hint is similar. Think of the day of the Last Judgment, and choose now what in that day will give you "greater joy and contentment." The idea is the same: my whole life before me, and this option set against the light of its background. Only here two touches are added: the view now is in the presence of God, from his angle and under his judgment; and then (because it is not the private judgment at the hour of death, but the public one of all mankind together in the last day that is envisaged), the view is also in the presence of the whole of mankind, witness and partner in the great act of the final end. My life, as background to my

103

choice, is now not only my own private affair, but the concern of God and the joint adventure of all men and women who closer or farther have touched my life, and I theirs, or have failed to do so when it should have been done. The picture for my discernment acquires now the dimension of obedience and submission to God whose child I am, and the dimension of solidarity with and accountability to all my brothers and sisters who walk with me and look at my final image together with me. An inspired setting for a choice.

And still a third hint, which Ignatius actually places first. To look at a person "whom I have never seen or known," and whose good I desire, and to imagine what I would advise him to do, in order myself to follow the advice I give to the other. Notice that it has to be a perfect stranger. A friend or even an acquaintance will not do. Ignatius is sparing of details, and when he does give them he means them. The idea, I understand, is that of gaining a fresh look at the question, to get a new angle, to look at it with a fresh eye. There is nothing that can foul up an election more effectively than a preconceived attitude, a prejudiced look, a routine approach. When routine presides over a choice, the decision is taken even before the question is formulated, and discernment dies before it has a chance to be born. And yet this is so very common with us that we instinctively refuse to see it and accept it. We let our choices be made for us by custom and tradition and sheer routine. The precedent in court. The repeated situation in life. And the repeated decision—which is most likely to be the wrong one because no situation is actually repeated in life. To allow the past to rule the present is to convert the present into the past, and that is cheating ourselves out of life which consists precisely and uniquely in the present. It is hard to make choices, as I have said in a full chapter earlier in this book, and a most popular escape from that painful task is the escape into history. Check the file, ask the previous incumbent, consult the past. What did we do in a similar situation? And do it again. It saves the trouble. And it kills the soul.

This is why we are asked now to look at a perfect stranger. Not even at a friend into whom we may project our own secret needs and wants out of familiarity and contact and affective identification. We are taken for a moment out of our world, almost out of our very person, and are asked to look at our problem from a distance. The important psychological distance. The perspective, the background, the setting, as in the two previous hints. And this time the point of the background is that it is not only actual but also new. No files, no references, no case history. Sharp outline and bold colors. Unexpected and surprising. To bring out the uniqueness of the situation and the originality of the choice. Landscape painters are said to look at the view they are painting, turned backwards, bent double, head down, peering uncomfortably through their own open legs. And that is simply to shake themselves out of the standard view that the upright position provides, to discover new angles, to let themselves be struck by nature in unusual perspectives, to discover the new in the old. And the Hindus, again, know and practice the ancient bodily wisdom of the headstand, straight as a pole with the legs up and head down, rerouting the currents of the body in yogic metabolism, while they look with mischievous ease on an upside-down world from an upsidedown view. That helps to straighten up things on the whole. Secret of art, of life and of choices. That is the approach. A fresh outlook provides a better frame for an independent appraisal—be it of colors and lines or of values and behavior. An important element in a good election is an unbiased, original, balanced view of the whole situation.

In fact when we speak impartially to another about a problem which he has and we too have, we are prone to tell him something different from what we tell our own selves about the same problem. More concretely, we tend to be more generous and broadminded with others than with ourselves. We know how to be kind and understanding with others, leaving the strictness and harshness and vindictiveness for ourselves. To speak to another, if only in imagination, can help broaden our views and soften our judgment.

On one occasion I remember, I was clearly helped in a decision by talking to another, not in fantasy but in real life. A religious superior in India consulted me once on the advisability of priests wearing a cassock. Now, I myself was a cassock addict. I hardly ever removed it except to go to bed at night, and had clung to it through all the heat and the monsoon and the awkwardness of tucking it up when pedaling on my cycle and the amused looks of people in the streets at my unusual garb which was wholly strange and meaningless to them. I knew that Catholics at large liked to see their priests clad in the white robe, and I took it as a symbol and witness and custodian of my own priestly role. As such I prized my white cassock, cherished it, took pride in it, kept it clean, and wore it faithfully in and out of the house throughout the day without fail. But when a superior in earnest asked my opinion, as a person being in touch with different types of social and religious groups in our region, and with a view to framing concrete directives for his subjects in the future, I found myself saying quite different things from what I had been telling myself about it. I mentioned how when I began to be invited to give talks to Hindu audiences I had often been put out by the giggling and open merriment of the public as I appeared onstage with the strange dress that meant nothing to them except something funny and outlandish. Though later I did come to know that the long dress meant after all something to them, and that not very complimentary either. As I learned the language and walked the streets I began to recognize the ribald words of abuse some people in small groups uttered toward me when I passed by them. In the varied and spicy vocabulary of backstage society they called me eunuch, homosexual, and transvestite. Fine witness was I bearing to the Catholic priesthood! All they saw in my beloved cassock was a man in woman's dress. A good piece of inculturation that was! I mentioned all that to the superior, as also the request I had received from a university colleague not to go to see him at his house so long as I wore that dress, as his neighbors believed he was being visited by a homosexual. I don't know what that good superior wrote in his report, but I do remember that a few days after speaking with him, when what I had told him had sunk into my own mind, I took action myself on my own; and one fine night I reverently folded my white cassock, kissed it and literally laid it down to rest. To speak to another about a situation that affected me too, had made me see more clearly in my own case.

These hints are valuable in themselves, and can be used on occasion with profit, but their deeper value lies in the principles they illustrate, the attitudes they stress, the atmosphere they create around a situation of choice. The impartial look, the balanced view, the totality of life, the presence of God, and the brotherly awareness of mankind standing by. These are not techniques to make a successful decision, but a climate, a culture, a spirituality to live in. And that is in fact the main point I'm driving at and want to get down to, the first idea in conceiving this book, and the sustained inspiration while writing it.

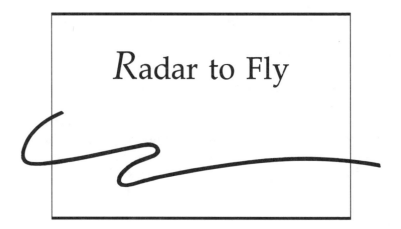

Radar to Fly

Among the happy moments of my life, free for the most part from great surprises, I count my unexpected meeting with J. Krishnamurti, a different thinker and a radical anti-guru whom I was privileged to meet a year before he died. I was waiting in the large hall of Madras Airport near the final gate, waiting for the announcement to board the flight to Bombay, when, in place of the expected announcement, the loudspeakers gave out a different kind of information, unfortunately not infrequent in my experience of airlines and airports: The flight would be delayed for an hour—no reason given—and we were to remain in the same hall till further notice. The inconvenience was regretted. There were looks of misery all around, a solitary murmur of mild protest, and finally a silent resignation to the unavoidable fate. We would wait. I let my face register annoyance in response to the common mood, and sat down to wait out the period of trial in my plastic seat. A modern version of medieval torture in aseptic surroundings. And then it happened. I lifted my eyes and looked straight in front of me. There he was. I had never seen him, but the photos I had seen and, even more, his unmistakable serenity and his quiet elegance identified his presence better than any visiting card. He was sitting just in front of me with a single companion by his side, in perfect anonymity in the midst of the hall packed with impatient travelers: A sense of peace in a tension of hurry. My reaction was instantaneous. I got up at once from my seat, came near to where he was, and, addressing his companion by his side I asked him respectfully, "May I speak for a moment to Mr. Krishnamurti?" I had spoken in a low tone but Krishnamurti heard me, and, before his companion could answer, he himself got up, joined his hands gracefully in answer to my already folded hands before him according to the beautiful Indian rubric, and then, unexpectedly, he took my hands between his and pressed and caressed them with a glowing warmth I had not expected from his books. I blurted out my thanks for the immense good his books had done for me; embarrassingly he tried to interrupt me, and, in that standing position, facing each other with swaying intertwined hands and delighted looks, we grew in fast intimacy as though we had known each other for life. He made me sit by his side, and I blessed, for once, the timely delay of the obliging plane. We had a full hour to ourselves.

This is not the place to chronicle that interview. However, I record here the most interesting moment of that spontaneous exchange, which surfaced in my memory as I was writing the last paragraph in the preceding chapter, almost asking to be here in its own right, however remote in time and mentality its relation to Ignatian themes would appear. When "K." (as he called himself, shortening his name in practical modesty to its briefest expression) realized that I was no casual admirer, much less a meddlesome interviewer, but a genuine seeker who knew well his writings and had a deep interest in them and in his person, he asked me a question that I myself, as a writer, like to ask when someone tells me he reads my books and I think I can expect from him

intelligent and useful feedback. He asked me, "What is it
that has struck you and helped you in my writings?" I was
ready with my answer. K. had been right in judging that I
had not spoken lightly, that I had read his works in detail
and had something to say about them and about what I had
learned from them. I spoke unhesitatingly while I felt the
ready approval in the welcoming features of his noble, hand-
some face turned toward me in exceptional concentration. I
said, "Three things I have learned in your writings,
Krishnaji. First, the effect of conditioning in our lives that
makes us conform blindly to accepted usage in thought and
behavior, makes us see what we do not see and be what we
are not; the slave situation you unmask with that virile
phrase of yours which has robbed me of my sleep more than
one night: 'We are second-hand people.' Second, the perni-
cious role fear plays in our lives as the most damaging and
most universal of emotions. And, third, the important and
practical principle that each problem has to be solved and
each decision has to be taken, not in its own narrow context
but in the larger frame of the totality of life: This vision of
totality is what gives balance to our feelings and clarity to
our view. That is my summary." K. smiled, visibly pleased,
and commented with humor: "When you told me you were
a Jesuit I was surprised to hear that a member of your order
read my books and liked them; but I am not surprised now at
the clear definiteness with which you sum up my thought."

The totality of life is the essential background for a right
choice. That is the comprehensive view of whatever one
knows and feels oneself to be from birth to death, in family
and in society, before oneself and before God, and in that
bird's-eye view one realizes at a glance whether this present
moment with its limited choice fits or not. The cosmic landscape of one's whole life as solemn backdrop to each single
choice. In that context, conditioning is all that—at least in
part and at least for a time—bends us, through an acquired

habit or an imposed custom, to what in genuine vocation and truthful existence we are not and do not want to be in our heart of hearts. And fear, finally, upsets the basic balance that our delicate organism requires for a proper choice. The elective process is essentially a removal of obstacles ("attachments," prejudices, conditionings) to achieve a balanced view, sharpen the conscience, and energize the senses to see all that is to be seen, to judge all that is to be judged, and to choose in freedom, with an almost inborn spontaneity, what has to be chosen against the existential background of the totality of life. No wonder K.'s descriptions of the fundamental activity of human choice sounded familiar to me, even through the filter of a different language, in expressing a basic attitude which coincides in essence with the religious detachment of the soul in search of the will of God in the midst of conditioning circumstances.

The same impression of walking a familiar landscape in a different climate came over me while reading the books of Carl Rogers, who has just as valid a claim to be mentioned here. The parallel with him is even more explicit, if possible. For him, the way to make proper decisions is to acquire first as much inner freedom as possible, liberating ourselves from all kinds of fears, phobias, prejudices, and complexes; and then to trust the spontaneous inclination of the total and responsible self before the alternatives at hand. Only the terminology changes. Instead of speaking of "the totality of life," Rogers speaks of "the whole organism," "the totality of the experience," "contact with reality as it is"; and instead of speaking of attachments he speaks of "complexes," but the basic process is the same. Information, contact, and balance. To see everything, to open all the windows, to consider all the data, to be in touch with all the aspects that come up and with all our feelings as those aspects come up; and then to maintain the neutral impartiality of the wise judge who has sifted through all the evidence and watches now the obvious conclusion emerge by itself, as it were, in the transparency of the peaceful mind. The wrong decision comes, says Rogers, when fear, prejudice, or passion close the windows of mind and senses, and thus the message gets blocked, mutilated, and garbled, and the center does not get the right information. Then, of course, the whole process is vitiated and decisions get inevitably misshaped. The channels of communication are obstructed, the wires get tangled, the signal confused, and the mind and the heart do not receive the reliable information they are entitled to. As a consequence they take the wrong course and reach the wrong conclusions. The organism is fine, but it had been fed the wrong information, and that accounts for the wrong conclusion. Again, it is not that the information was not there, but that it did not reach its destination: I knew the fact, but my fear did not allow it to register clearly in my conscience when it should have been there. I was not open, balanced, "indifferent," and my subconscious did not allow the message to get through. Subconscious fears are the greatest cause of misguided decisions. On the contrary, the fearless contact of the whole of a person with the whole of reality is the ideal situation for a proper election.

In Rogers' words, "The person under therapy increasingly discovers that his own organism is trustworthy, that it is a suitable instrument for discovering the most satisfactory behavior in each immediate situation. To the extent that this person is open to all of his experience, he has access to all of the available data in the situation on which to base his behavior. He has knowledge of his own feelings and impulses, which are often complex and contradictory. He is freely able to sense the social demands. He has access to his memories of similar situations, and the consequences of different behaviors in those situations. He is better able to permit his total organism, his conscious thought participating, to consider, weigh and balance each stimulus, need and demand,

and its relative weight and intensity. The defects which interfere with this weighing and balancing are that we include things that are not a part of our experience, and exclude elements which are."

In another remarkable paragraph Rogers expresses the basis of his characteristic optimism: "One of the most revolutionary concepts to grow out of our clinical experience is the growing recognition that the innermost core of man's nature, the deepest layers of his personality, the base of his 'animal nature,' is positive in nature—is basically socialized, forward-moving, rational and realistic. . . . When man's unique capacity of awareness is functioning freely and fully, we find that we have, not an animal whom we must fear, not a beast who must be controlled, but an organism able to achieve, through the remarkable integrative capacity of its central nervous system, a balanced, realistic, self-enhancing, other-enhancing behavior as a resultant of all these elements of awareness. To put it another way, when man is less than fully man—when he denies to awareness various aspects of his experience—then indeed we have all too often reason to fear him and his behavior, as the present world situation testifies. But when he is most fully man, when he is his complete organism, when awareness of experience, that peculiarly human attribute, is most fully operating, then he is to be trusted, then his behavior is constructive" *(On Becoming a Person).* This is a psychologist speaking in professional language, but a psychologist of whom Fritz Perls, with good-humored jealousy, said, "Carl Rogers is a saint."

I am not so naive as to propose that Carl Rogers, Krishnamurti, and St. Ignatius are saying exactly the same thing. My only purpose is to bring to light the remarkable coincidence of the basic accord three thinkers, from considerably different backgrounds, on the fundamental point of decision-making on which the whole of life depends. It has been my own personal and pleasurable experience that, in

113

quite different periods and circumstances of my life, these three independent thinkers have enlightened me and confirmed me in this elementary method of reacting to life, which I want to set out in this book as the center and marrow of healthy and holy living. I summarize it here once again: First, liberation from all that can vitiate the choice, in order to achieve, as far as humanly possible, the transparency and openness of the clear sky and the tranquil sea in limitless horizon; the contact then with all that can be relevant to the choice, in message and feeling, for today and for tomorrow, with the soul at peace with itself and with God, the core and basis of that total reality of which we form part as we shape our lives; and, finally, trust in ourselves and in God who guides us, to open the windows of the mind, let it favor the instinctive choice, and then embrace that choice with joy. This is the way of wise and holy men.

My favorite comparison is the radar screen. The circular vigil, the constant watch around 360 degrees, not sparing any angle in the persevering search. The ruthlessly impartial ray of light that sweeps the heavens at measured intervals, denouncing instantly the presence of any new object on the horizons of consciousness. And then the expert identification, the instant reaction, the exact turn at the precise moment, that opens up the sure way in the dark night of our human existence. A good radar to help us fly in safety.

The Day
in the Spirit

Once in a group of friends we proposed that each would tell the others how he went about finding the will of God and making decisions in his life. There was freedom, intimacy, and warmth between all, and we expected all of us to gain spiritual insight both by telling and by listening to each other's experiences in cordial exchange. We did. We learned from each other. And one unexpected thing I learned was how restricted the scope of making choices was for many, how little the art of discernment was practiced, what a small space the conscious exercise of decision in the Spirit had in most people's lives. What I mean is, more clearly, that, in this exchange, most people restricted the examples they gave to big things in life, to extraordinary occasions and trying circumstances when they had a difficult and important choice to make. They spoke on how they chose to become religious, to come to the missions, to decide on a line of work (and these are perfectly legitimate examples, and I've given my own experience of those fundamental choices in my life in this very book); but what shocked me was that nobody spoke on making decisions and finding the will of God in small things, in daily things, in the constant run of life and the continuous flow of events that make up our existence. As though elections were, much like political elections in a democracy, something to be practiced only from time to time, every four or five years according to the constitution of the country, on a special occasion, after a long process and with an extraordinary effort after which one has to rest again till the next unavoidable big event. That was the impression —and for me the shock—caused by the way my spiritual friends spoke on that day. I want to analyze that situation.

Elections are certainly for the big things. No doubt about it. But they are for very much more in life, and that is what makes their study worthwhile and their practice rewarding. I shall say it plainly: If discernment and elections were only for the big events, I wouldn't have written this book. To provide guidelines for rare exceptional occasions does not attract me, nor inspire me to write a book and put myself into it as I like to do when I write. But I consider that this matter of making choices is the very texture of life, the mood of the soul and the temper of the spirit; it is a permanent state and a defining attitude, and as such is worthy of full attention and deep study. For me the art of choosing is the art of living, because life is made up of choices. That is what makes life what it is. My choices are what I am. All of them. The big dilemmas and the small options, the heroic determinations and the spontaneous likings, the big jumps and the small steps. And the small steps are many more in number than the big jumps.

A similar misunderstanding prevails with many in the way of interpreting Ignatius' Exercises. As they seem to be centered on the "election of a state of life," they are often considered as just a procedure for a young man or woman to decide whether he or she wants to marry or become a priest or a religious. Thus understood, the Exercises are, to be sure, an efficient tool for decision in that important moment of

life, but then they would cease to be of any use outside that
concrete and limited scope. The Exercises are not meant to
decide an election, but to create a context within which an
election can be made, to provide the favorable atmospheric
conditions for the right choice, for any choice at any time;
and to make us live in a constant state of awareness and
discernment that will easily lead us to choose paths and take
turns wherever we are and whenever we need it. That is
their importance, and that is their usefulness. They are not a
manual to make decisions, not an election procedure, not a
set of rules and rubrics; but an environment, a milieu, a spirituality, a frame of mind in which to live and breathe and
move and find one's way and reach one's goal. Once the big
decision has been made, ideally in such a setting as the Exercises provide, that fundamental election has to be carried out
in the small daily choices that are its consequence and its
expression and its practical application: they too need that
guidance and discernment and strength. To provide that
there are the repeated Exercises year after year, and even
more day by day, which—in their prolonged action and sustained effect—guide and prompt and sustain and lead us. To
consider the Exercises as Ignatius' tool to pull in followers is
to debase them. As a matter of history, Peter Favre made
them two years after his decision to follow Ignatius, and
Francis Xavier after the very vow that united the first pre-
jesuits at Montmartre. The Exercises are a help in finding the
will of God; and to find the will of God, I repeat with Ignatius, is to find God. Thus they are a school of prayer, of faith,
of discernment, of love. They are meant to cover the whole
of life—in length and in depth.

I heard Fr. Arrupe say in an inspired homily to a group of
young Jesuits in Goa before the exposed remains of St. Francis Xavier: "A Jesuit is a man who lives in a state of election." A beautiful definition. In my desire to reach all priests
and religious and all men and women who walk the paths of

the Spirit, I feel justified in replacing "Jesuit" with any other religious appellation, or rather, universally, with the most general term, and say: "A Christian is a person who lives in a state of election." Though, there again, I live among Hindus and Muslims and Parsis and Jains, and feel impelled to enlarge the scope even more and include them too in the basic definition, though I can't find the phrase. That is the problem of genuine universal ecumenism. My problem. Let us say that the religious person is one who lives in a state of election. That is the crucial point. The state, the process, the continuity. The readiness, the alertness, the preparedness. The rules and procedures and hints and considerations assimilated, integrated, vivified, and made practical reality in the multiple choices of the day. The whole life made into a continued election. The contact, the balance, the confirmation, the generosity. Every nerve tuned and every muscle tempered. And then we move into life and face its thousand situations. An option confronts us. Which way to take? And the personal spiritual computer blinks into action. This way, please. And we step on. Simple. Natural. Spontaneous. Each choice becomes a satisfaction in itself and a preparation for the next one. It tones up the machine and keeps it ready. Next option. This way. A more important decision. We're ready for it. A simple one. We take it in our stride, but aware and conscious that we are making a choice. Always on line. This may mean changing direction at every turn. The constant consciousness that we are making our way and finding our path and living our life. We know the responsibility and the enjoyment of the driver who scans the road and senses the break and touches the wheel gently or turns it firmly as he picks his way and joins the traffic and judges speed and distance and curve and horizon, and steers his vehicle safe and steady, a decision at every instant, a choice every second in the grip of his hands, a happy journey, a joyful time. We are in the driver's seat. Let us enjoy the driving.

The Day in the Spirit

To extend the practice of discernment to the whole day, Ignatius uses a method which has come to characterize his spirituality: the examination of conscience. Twice a day for a quarter of an hour, another quarter of an hour after each meditation, and the constant vigilance of the "particular examen" throughout the day, with detailed legislation right at the opening of the Exercises and unremitting insistence through them as well as in the "Constitutions" and in his correspondence and his personal practice. It is known that Ignatius never dispensed any of his subjects from the practice of the daily examination of conscience. He would permit a sick man, and at times even a busy man or an earnest student, to omit his prayer, but never his examination of conscience. Such insistence has caused surprise in some, and even opposition and rejection at times. A serious Jesuit, since appointed to responsible formation jobs, told me once personally: "When I came to know this exaggerated insistence on such a mechanical practice as the examination of conscience, I lost all respect for St. Ignatius." If there were any question of a mechanical practice, he would have had reason for his distaste. But there could be nothing more distant from Ignatius' idea than a rigid procedure, a spiritual bookkeeping, a glorified stocktaking, an audit, a graph, a questionnaire. "The examen in Ignatius is, first and foremost, a state of the spirit; that is, a general disposition of that makes him be constantly watchful and keen to know and discern the movements of the spirit, and consequently to adapt his reactions and direct his behavior. If this constant awareness is there, the actual mechanics of the examen are not essential," says such a traditional interpreter as Casanovas. That is the attitude. A watch, a consciousness, a regard. A line, a direction, a mood. Actually it is not fifteen minutes but twenty-four hours that the examen should last. The fifteen minutes are a useful reminder, a sharpening of the attention and a deepening of the sense, a highlight, a crest, a peak. But the state of the soul continues. As a fine musician, although not composing music all the time, nonetheless all the time *is* a musician, a composer, an artist; and tunes and rhythms and notes and melodies run in his head, ready to spring into score when the moment strikes. The actual composing reinforces the mood, and the mood prevails and subsists and underlies all activities at all times. Mozart was always Mozart.

Ignatius was always Ignatius. And there is a telling testimony to show that this was the way he himself understood and practiced his maligned examen. The witness is tucked away in the pages of his journal, where the entry for 19th February 1544 begins: "On awakening in the morning and beginning my examination of conscience. . . ." Nice way to begin the day: by making an examination of conscience. (I hope my objector friend doesn't hear of it!) What was that holy old man examining on waking up in the morning? His dreams? He was no Freudian. His behavior? Sleep spreads a daily merciful moratorium on our conscience. We don't sin while we snore. No, he was not examining virtues and vices. He was finding himself. He had made his last examen when going to bed the previous night, and now resumes his practice as soon as he wakes up in the morning, because for him the examen was the way to be himself, to get in touch, to be aware, to be sensitive, to be fully conscious, to feel God's presence, to discern his will, to find his ways, to order his day, to make the decisions a "general" had to make, to check his path, to live his life. First thing in the morning. Last thing at night. And therefore every single thing in between, big and small, transient or permanent, deep or shallow, every event and every word and every look and every response discerned and oriented and directed and "examined," not in the cold wires of an electronic circuit, but in the beating heart of a living man who knew himself to live all the time before his living God.

The Day in the Spirit

From morning to night. The outline of a day in the Spirit: Getting up with a sense of expectation. What will God have ready for me today? What will he tell me? How will he lead me? What will be the important moments of the day, the crossroads, the encounters, the signposts? He who expects nothing, sees nothing. Dullness of mind is mankind's favorite sickness. Nothing happens because nothing is expected to happen, life doesn't take off because the owner of that life doesn't believe it can ever take off, days are sheer routine because that is what the administrator of that day means it to be. What can ever happen in a world of clerks and accountants and shopkeepers? With my full respects to those who make their living in a shop or in an office, that is not for life in the Spirit and joy in his breath. Nothing happens to most people because most people don't have the creativity and sensitivity and liberty to let things happen. Blessed are those who expect nothing, because they will not be disappointed. Beatitude of death. Graveyard stillness. Why be born for that? Scan the horizon to spot the birds. Train your ears to detect the music. Wake up each day with a sense of newness, of keenness, of readiness for life in its daily freshness and fragrance and light. No two sunrises are equal.

Then prayer presides over the day. And prayer is again facing the ever new and ever different face of God. Prayer is listening and watching and contemplating. Contemplation which, again in Ignatius' practice, was contemplation in action, and in my understanding too, contemplation *for* action. To receive on the mountain the guidelines for the journey, the strategy for the battle. The briefing, the planning, the encouragement. The report, the secret messages, the intelligence. And then every skirmish is a surprise. Every move a novelty. To be sensed and treasured and enjoyed. The mood of the day to be captured in prayer as preparation and setting, as a background to the choices that will make up the day. Set the focus before calling the shots.

The Art of Choosing

The Eucharist, irrespective of the time of day it is celebrated, is the highlight of this daily contact with God, as of
everything else indeed. "To go up to the Temple," "to enter
the Lord's presence," were already—in Old Testament language—expressions to mean finding the will of God and
making decisions. We enter the presence of the King to receive orders and to get directives. And he gives them. The
purification rite that opens the eucharistic celebration re-
stores balance to our heart and clarity to our sight. The stage
is ready. Praise and adoration in song and glory prepare the
soul for the majesty of the presence. And then God speaks.
The readings of the day are not just passages fixed by a
remote routine printed years before in a rigid calendar of
ancient rubrics; each reading is new and actual and present,
if only we can listen to it with a fresh ear and a living faith;
that is, listen to God in it today, and God speaking to me.
The Bible is not a record of files or tapes containing old
oracles for convenient replay before a pious audience. No.
Each reading from the stand at the common celebration is a
direct confrontation, a personal encounter, an inspiration
and a command. And our answer, in gesture of bread and
wine, and in prayer of dedication and sanctification, is our
self-offering, our surrender, our Yes of today, actualizing and
concretizing our lifelong consecration to God and bringing it
to bear on the twenty-four hours that follow. The meal in
common seals our commitment, and in its strength we go to
carry out, in the thousand "elections" of the day, the fundamental choice we have renewed at the altar.

And now the day itself for which we have risen and
prayed and dreamed. The will of God begins to take shape
for today. Events and news and meetings and work. Each
person I meet brings with him- or herself a measure of subtle
choices. Shall I greet him, shall I stop to talk, shall I be long,
shall I be formal, shall I confide, shall I avoid, shall I show
interest, shall I show love? A thousand choices in a chance

meeting—if only I'm alive to them and welcome them and make them with conscious ease as I go along noticing persons and things and events, and reacting to them in constant awareness and joyful freedom. If I miss those choices, my life becomes routine, and I just keep saying the same things to the same people at the same time in the same place. And doing the same things in the same way with the same boredom. But if I notice the subtle difference of each day and adjust my reactions to the changing tune, the faces, the looks, the eyes, the smile, the playing shadows and the dancing breeze, then I spring to life and notice and enjoy myself and become myself and contribute to liberating the world around me from the chains and fetters of deadly routine.

Now and then the big occasion. An important choice, a doubt, a decision. And I positively enjoy it because I'm trained to do it and ready to do it, and know that by doing it I grow under grace and come closer to God and shape my life to his honor and glory. I call the alert, I sharpen my senses, I set the process in motion. The machinery is ready. The reasons, the advice, the mixed motives, the foreseeable consequences. And deeper down the lead of the Spirit, the gentle persuasion, the mysterious attraction, and the clarity, the peace, the joy that signal God's good pleasure and mark the way and invite the step. I wait. I don't hurry. And I don't delay. Each choice has its moment in the stars when it fits and prospers and begets life. I sense the fullness of time surging up within me. I yield to the tide. I nod my head gently. I make my choice. I give my Yes. I offer it to God. He also nods. We understand each other. And I go ahead joyful and strengthened with the vital experience of a personal election. The day has been redeemed.

Of course I make mistakes. Though I don't call a choice wrong simply because it turns out badly. Maybe at the moment I made the decision, that was the right decision given the information I had; but then events took another turn and my choice proved unfortunate in the end. Fine. The result was unpleasant, but the process was valid. Like a game that brings with itself the reward of playing, even if the final score is not favorable to me. The referee signals the defeat. But it has been a good game, and I've enjoyed every bit of it. And so I learn. I take full responsibility for my decisions and whatever outcomes they bring. I don't blame circumstances or the weather or a bad stomach or incompetent advisers or God or the devil, not even the government. And I don't blame myself. I do go through the process again to understand what happened—and I realize I am making my "examen!" Wholesome practice.

There are blackouts too. Nothing comes through. The line is out. No guidance, no mood, no direction, no way, no singing of the birds and no window in the black sky. The earth is made of lead, and life is a burden. Then I remind myself, though even to do that is painful and I have to do it almost forcibly, that silence also speaks and darkness has a message, that if I depend on God for my guidance and counsel, I have to respect him as he is, to let him deal with me as he thinks best, to let him be himself with me. And if he chooses to be silent, I will worship a silent God and increase my vigilance and use my lights and feel my way, knowing all the time that he is there and watches my step and will unexpectedly show his light at a turn of the way—provided I keep walking.

Night comes to close the day. The last look back. The taking in of the day's experience in grateful review. The lowering of the flag, letting the will relax and responsibility have its break. No choices through the night. Only to be ready tomorrow when the cock crows and dawn bursts into my eyes. "On waking up and beginning my examination of conscience. . . ." Life goes on, because the making of choices goes on. Welcome to a new day.

124

Friendship
with Creation

The following story may, at first sight, look out of place. But it has a message and it belongs right here. I'll make that clear at once. The story concerns one of the loveliest saints of our time, Swami Ramdas. The unassuming clerk who turned to God, left everything, went to that home of ascetics and land of mystics which is the Himalayas, experienced God with all the fullness mortal man is capable of, and came back to share in wisdom and wit his vision of God with men on the plains of life. Now, this Ramdas, before the uprooting experience that changed his life, was a smoker. He didn't smoke any expensive brand, but the popular *"bidi,"* the small, short, single filled-up leaf loosely rolled onto itself and tied with an uncouth thread around the middle to keep it in its slightly conical shape. The common man's smoke. The "roll," which is what "bidi" means. The cheapest addiction in India. Ramdas had it too. Till God struck, and then, with many other more important things in his life, the bidi just disappeared into oblivion. No smoking in the Himalayas. Years passed and life mellowed for Ramdas, and then he himself charmingly tells how in later years, safe in the ashram he had founded, and in the love and care of his disciples, he would occasionally, of a rare day, in a special celebration, ask for a bidi, take it, light it, and smoke it slowly in happy contentment, enjoying the simplest of pleasures with unfeigned innocence.

The point of the story? Not precisely to justify smoking. If anyone wants to use Swami Ramdas' example to defend his own brand of cigarettes, he'll have to go to the Himalayas first. The point is quite another. The point is to mark the difference between the "bidis" before and the "bidis" after, with the Himalayas in between. They may have been the same brand, the same length, the same price—and yet they were entirely and radically different. The bidi smoked in his office as a clerk was the smoke of addiction, of compulsion, of necessity; bondage, slavery, and jail. A chain smoker does not enjoy his smoke. He needs it, he wants it, he cannot do without it. But he doesn't relish it. He hardly even notices anymore when he is smoking; he only notices when he doesn't. He misses his smoke when he stops, and craves it again. That is to satisfy a need, but it cannot be called enjoyment. An alcoholic will drink anything to calm the desperate thirst of his whole body. Even French polish or methylated spirits. There is no taste in the bottle. No pleasure in the needle. Only the imperative need to satisfy in any way an inner craving beyond all control. Such were the bidis Ramdas had smoked in addiction. But the occasional bidi he smoked after years of penance and abstinence and purification and liberation, after regaining the balance of life and the use of the senses and the nearness of nature, was a bidi smoked in freedom. And that made all the difference. That brought out the taste, the relaxation, the gentle intoxication, the brotherhood with smoking humanity, and the innocent mischief of doing publicly what a holy man is not supposed to do—and getting away with it. All that was certainly worth a smoke. And Ramdas enjoyed it to the full.

And now the point of the story. What has it to do with choices and with Ignatius and with the point of this whole book? Quite a good deal. The purpose of life is to make the right choices, and the obstacle to the right choices are the "attachments," the "creatures" (again Ignatius' term) that lure us away from the right path and make us take the wrong turn and miss our goal. Hence the constant watch, the mistrust, the going to "the other end of the diameter," the open battle, the unremitting fight. We against the world. Is that enmity to last forever? No. We can make peace and sign a treaty and enjoy its benefits and the beauty of creation. And that is what Ignatius does at the end of his month-long Exercises. After the purification of the First Week, the formal "elections" of the Second, the "confirmation" of the election with the suffering Christ in the Third Week, and the joy of his resurrection in the Fourth, Ignatius has a final lesson ready before letting the disciple out into the world again. And that lesson is precisely the reconciliation with all that is —even the "creatures" that could lead us astray. He gives a beautiful name to that final lesson: Contemplation to Obtain Love. And this is its teaching.

The contemplation opens with an act of universal thanksgiving. It is precisely through thanksgiving that reconciliation with creation takes place. That is a Pauline idea. "For every creature of God is good, and nothing is to be rejected that is accepted with thanksgiving" (1 Tim. 4:4). Creation was dangerous when attachment to it endangered the purity of our choices. Now after the purification of repentance, indifference, suffering, surrender, commitment to Christ, and love without end, creation becomes friendly and the earth becomes a home. The "creatures" have been tamed, the sting has been removed, the air has been cleared, the toys can be given back to the child to play with. The man of God can smoke again.

Friendliness with creation is the condition of a happy life, and as such is the right background on which to project the mapping of our ways and the planning of our lives. If a person believes himself to be in enemy territory, his choice of route will be severely limited and conditioned by the fear of being discovered and captured. He will avoid main streets and highways, will have to tread along hidden paths and backyard alleys, and in any case will not enjoy his wanderings. But if a person knows himself to be in his own country, his familiar surroundings and his beloved landscape, he is at liberty to choose any path and walk any street and trample along any road or just open country. He has the choice of the land before him. And we have the choice of the whole of creation that is placed before us by a loving Father, for us to accept and enjoy in grateful freedom. Our choices are as wide as the universe. And that is our greatness.

This friendly relationship is increased (still following Ignatius in his parting thoughts) by the fact that God himself dwells in his gift. He is present in nature, "in plants and animals and men and all elements" and operates in them their very being, "their growing and acting and helping me." Our aim was and is "to find God in all things," and he is literally there, surrounding us in "the new heaven and the earth" that are his dwelling and consequently our home. And again "to find God in all things" means for us in practice "to find the will of God always," and that is the happy exercise of our love and our faith in the lovely surroundings of a friendly world. If constant awareness is the way to health and contemplation and fulfillment, we have before us a "divinized awareness" that, if practiced in faith, can change our lives. God is near, and his paths are open to us.

God is not only near, but within us, closer to us than our own heart. "He is in me giving me life and sense and understanding . . . making me into his own temple." God lives in me, works in me, loves in me, and, in the language I am using of life and choices and the equation between them,

God chooses in me. That is the climax of the "elections." I sense his presence, know his tastes, feel his inclinations, and just yield in the center of my soul to the promptings of his Spirit. "Be it done unto me." Let him do, let him move, let him choose. That is the summary of the whole process, the end of the thirty days, the fulfillment of a person's life. God acts in me. Christ lives in me. He knows the Father's will, and in his love and care will gently work it out in me. That is my faith.

I love doing exegesis, and I'm going to indulge in a bit of it on a text of the Exercises. Ignatius measured his words and spared his grammar, and when an expression of his is repeated in different contexts, it points to an important idea, a basic principle, a key concept in his understanding of the ways of the Spirit. The expression that concerns me here is "comes from above." It appears first in the texts of the "elections," and I remember having quoted it there when Ignatius says that "the love that moves me to make this particular choice must come from above." It is repeated in another election context, when Ignatius gives advice to regulate the giving of alms, how much and to whom, and begins by saying: "The first rule is that the love that moves me and makes me give this alms should come from above." And the third time the phrase appears in Ignatius' text is in the last paragraph of this last consideration on love. "To see how all that I have and own comes from above, as my limited power from the supreme and infinite power that is above . . . as the rays from the sun and the waters from the source." "Coming from above." That is the password. When choosing and when living and when being. "From above." The phrase has biblical coinage: "All good present, and every perfect gift, comes from above, from the Father of the lights in heaven. With him there is no variation, no play of passing shadows" (James 1:17). And, interestingly, James' vocabulary in that quotation is the vocabulary of astronomy and movement of the stars in the heavens which guided the paths of the ancients. All comes from above. The most secret movement within me, the lights and the shadows, the impulses of my heart and the orbits of my thought, all come from above, from the Father of lights in heaven. My breath becomes sacred. My thoughts become theology. My choices become the pulse of God beating in me through the daily life of my doubts and my decisions and my circumstances and my solutions. All coming from above. Practical mysticism. Prayerful management. The Spirit and the computer. Contemplation in action. A whole spirituality in that little phrase. A whole program of life in that pregnant sentence. "Coming from above." The art now is to experience it in full while we still are here below.

In Rabindranath Tagore's prayer:

It shall be my endeavour to reveal thee in my
    actions—knowing it is thy power gives me strength
    to act.

Life of my life, I shall ever try to keep my body
    pure—knowing that your living touch is upon all my
    limbs.

I shall ever try to keep all untruths out of my
    thoughts—knowing that thou art that truth which
    has kindled the light of reason in my mind.

I shall ever try to drive all evils away from my heart
    and keep it in flower—knowing that thou hast thy
    seat in the inmost shrine of my heart

The Cloud
of Knowing

A reading from the Book of Numbers (9:15–23):

"On the day when they set up the Tabernacle, that is the Tent of the Tokens, cloud covered it, and in the evening a brightness like fire appeared over it till the morning. So it continued: the cloud covered it by day and a brightness like fire by night. Whenever the cloud lifted from the tent, the Israelites struck camp, and at the place where the cloud settled, there they pitched their camp. At the command of the Lord they struck camp, and at the command of the Lord then encamped again, and continued in camp as long as the cloud rested over the Tabernacle. When the cloud stayed long over the Tabernacle, the Israelites remained in attendance on the Lord and did not move on; and it was the same when the cloud continued over the Tabernacle only a few days: at the command of the Lord they remained in camp, and at the command of the Lord they struck camp. There were also times when the cloud continued only from evening till morning, and in the morning, when the cloud lifted, they moved on. Whether by day or by night, they moved as soon as the cloud lifted. Whether it was for a day or two, for a month or a year, whenever the cloud stayed long over the Tabernacle, the Israelites remained where they were and did not move on; they did so only when the cloud lifted. At the command of the Lord they encamped, and at his command they struck camp. At the Lord's command, given through Moses, they remained in attendance on the Lord."

The Cloud.

The presence, the comfort, the guidance.

The direction to tell where to go, and the command to fix how long to stay.

Israel will not move so long as the cloud does not move, but will swiftly strike camp and lift the tents and pack the tabernacle and load the asses and move in a body through the trackless sand as soon as the cloud begins to lift.

The people that follow the cloud.

That is the people of God.

That is us.

Forty years.

That is a lifetime.

Through the desert.

That is life.

The cloud is free, unpredictable, surprising.

Nobody knows which way it will go or how long it will stay. Its path is no highway, and its wanderings are not in any map. Start and go. Move and follow. A whole people. And mankind's history with them.

The cloud has settled.

The people rest.

They haven't chosen the spot, but they take it and accept it, they explore its surroundings and search for its resources. Is there water near? Any trees? Grass for the cattle? Game for food? How are the approaches of the land? Where to set up guards, where to take refuge in an enemy raid? By now they are experts in survival, and can tap any resource and profit by any circumstance. They can turn any root into food and any ravine into a shelter. They can even draw water from a rock. Moses did.

Sometimes the people grumble.

As we do.

Why this spot, why this food, why this way?

Why?

The question that brings its punishment with itself.

Unrest, complaint, rebellion.

And plague strikes and the earth opens and the Levites ply the sword.

Israel learns slowly the ways of God.

As we do.

And they worship in the desert.

As we do.

The people stay and wonder. The cloud doesn't move. How long still in this place? It's no summer resort, and we seem to be stuck here. Months have passed. How many, who remembers? When did we settle here? Seems ages now. But the cloud doesn't budge. Weren't we supposed to reach a promised land? And can we reach it if we don't move? But the cloud doesn't seem to care. It has struck root in the soil like a tree. People have been conceived and have been born here, the span of mortal man in his mother's womb. And the cloud doesn't move. Four seasons have passed. Thinking every day will be the last. Wishing every morning the cloud would lift. But it doesn't. It stays. And the people with it. Some even die there. And are buried in the transient sand.

And then one day . . .

A shout rends the sky and reverberates in the desert.

The cloud is up!
All jump out to see.
All eyes converge on high.
People will tell each other for days who was the first to see it.
All see the forgotten miracle.
It moves!
The cloud is on the move.
And the people with it.
One whole year is a long time, and wells had been dug and shelters had been built and boundaries had been marked. All is left in an instant. The cloud has moved, and Israel is on its feet. Instant obedience. Total readiness.
Each day, ready to move.
Each day, ready to stay.
That is life in the Spirit.
That is Israel's boast.
And the whole people, leaving their dead and taking their newborn, move in the new direction with a new hope.

New halt.
How long?
Get ready for another year, people say. Dig your trenches and build your enclosures. This is a slow march. We are getting experience. We'll make sure we have a good camp this time. We'll begin work tomorrow.
Tomorrow?
Before the sun is up, the shout again:
The cloud!!!
It's up again!
But it cannot be! We've hardly settled here. It's only one night. What's that cloud up to? Playing with us? Joking? Enjoying itself? Can't it be sensible, predictable, consistent? Sometimes it's one year, and sometimes it's one day. No one

can tell. Even Moses has no explanations to offer. And all must obey. Up with everything. Forgo plans. Shake laziness away. Tie up what you untied last night. And move fast ahead. The cloud is gaining ground. We can't afford to miss it. For all its whims we depend on it and we want it and we love it.

But one thing.
Have you noticed the cloud's direction?
It seems to be retracing its steps.
We came that way.
And now it goes back the way it came.
Any sense in that?
Don't stop to ask, or you'll lose sight of it. Get up, start going, and don't ask questions. Your only duty is to follow. Go ahead, and never mind when you reach it or where.
That crazy cloud.
It starts, it stops, it stays, it moves.
It advances, retreats, goes around, retraces its steps.
Is that a way to reach anywhere?
In forty desert years nobody knew what it would do next. They must have talked a lot among themselves, those Israelites, about the cloud. Or maybe they didn't. Because they knew the mystery and sensed the presence. And they followed and accepted and obeyed. Ready to start. Ready to stop. Their eyes on the cloud. Their bodies accustomed to its nearness. Their feet eager to follow its lead.

The cloud.
The Spirit.
Fidelity and loyalty and docility.
Symbol and reality; promise and truth; history and reality.

We are the people of the cloud.

Discernment, decisions, choices, elections.

Challenge, purification, commitment, confirmation.

Image and fact. Tradition and experience. Prophecy and fulfillment.

To learn the ways of the Spirit, and to follow the wanderings of the cloud. Every mystic will speak of it. Every Christian will understand it. Every spiritual person will live it. We are the people that follow the cloud.

Faith and hope.

Indifference and detachment.

Balance and perspective.

The trial and the doubts and the victory.

All through life, day and night, in long patience and daily joy. Singing psalms, blowing trumpets, crossing rivers, and fighting battles. With slavery left behind, freedom conquered, a desert made friendly, and a horizon to scan with hope.

Because beyond those mountains lies the Promised Land.

End of the Book of Exodus (40:36–38):

"At every stage of their journey, when the cloud lifted from the Tabernacle, the Israelites broke camp; but if the cloud did not lift from the Tabernacle, they did not break camp until the day it lifted. For the cloud of the Lord hovered over the Tabernacle by day, and there was fire in the cloud by night, and the Israelites could see it at every stage of their journey."

Which is ours.